make ahead
BREAD

make ahead BREAD

100 Recipes for Melt-in-Your-Mouth Fresh Bread Every Day

Plus **Butters & Spreads**

Donna Currie

Photography by **Kate Sears**

The Taunton Press

for Bob

The Taunton Press
Inspiration for hands-on living®

THE TAUNTON PRESS, INC.
63 South Main Street
PO Box 5506
Newtown, CT 06470-5506
e-mail: tp@

EDITOR: **Carolyn Mandarano**
COPY EDITOR: **Nina Rynd Whitnah**
INDEXER: **Heidi Blough**
COVER AND INTERIOR DESIGN: **carol singer|notice design**
LAYOUT: **carol singer|notice design**
ART DIRECTOR: **Rosalind Loeb Wanke**
PHOTO EDITOR: **Erin Giunta**
PHOTOGRAPHER: **Kate Sears/Carol Myers Reps**
COVER PHOTOGRAPHER: **Kate Sears**
FOOD STYLIST: **Joyce Sangirardi/Carol Myers Reps**
PROP STYLIST: **Kate Parisian/Carol Myers Reps**

Library of Congress Cataloging-in-Publication Data

Currie, Donna.
  Make ahead bread : 100 recipes for bake-it-when-you-want-it yeast breads / Donna Currie.
    pages cm
  Summary: "This book created in a two-part approach that both saves time and enhances flavor, the recipes in Make Ahead Bread will give inexperienced bakers and busy home cooks the information they need to make bread on a schedule that works for them"-- Provided by publisher.
  ISBN 978-1-62710-395-4 (paperback)
  1. Bread. 2. Make-ahead cooking. I. Title.
  TX769.C848 2014
  641.81'5--dc23
                        2014027336

PRINTED IN THE UNITED STATES OF AMERICA
10 9 8 7 6 5 4 3 2 1

ACKNOWLEDGMENTS

MANY PEOPLE CONTRIBUTED to the creation of this book, perhaps starting with Adam Kuban, who gave me a bread-baking column on *Serious Eats* that got me on a roll. Casey Benedict mentioned my name in the right place at the right time and my agent, Holly Schmidt, nudged and prodded me and kept me from loafing too much.

The whole team at Taunton has been a pleasure to work with, from Carolyn Mandarano to the folks who handled the photos to the publicity folks. It's been a great challenge and a heck of a lot of fun.

I'd be remiss if I didn't mention my cheering squad at The Water Cooler, and the past and present members of Virtual Potluck, 37 Cooks, and Sunday Supper. There are way too many bloggers to mention individually, all of whom encouraged me, cheered for me, made me laugh, and sometimes gave me a well-needed reality check.

Carla Gonzales at Good Cook™ deserves a special mention. I don't think I can count how many times she'd call and say, "What are you doing now?" even though she knew the answer was "baking bread." Besides cheering me on and helping me brainstorm a few recipes, she also sent loaf pans, baking pans, and baking sheets to make sure my oven, refrigerator, kitchen counters, and dining room table were always full of bread in some stage of progress.

A special thanks to Sandra Simmons, who quietly stepped in and took over my blog, Cookistry, for a month when I really needed the help. And thanks to all the bloggers who helped her help me. Sometimes it takes a virtual village.

There are a lot of companies who directly and indirectly helped with the production of this book, whether by sending samples, providing information, or just making products that made my work so much easier. Those include the following: King Arthur® Flour, Red Star® Yeast, KitchenAid®, Challenge Butter®, Wüstoff®, Hodgson Mill®, Magimix®, Land O'Lakes™, Bob's Red Mill®, Brod & Taylor®, Good Cook, and Cuisinart®.

My greatest cheerleader throughout this project—and throughout our lives—is my husband. When he became ill and was hospitalized, drugged, groggy, incoherent, and possibly delirious, he was still telling people about my cooking and handing out business cards for my blog. He sampled more bread than he wanted to, critiqued the results, and gathered up loaves and buns and flatbreads and delivered them to friends, family, and co-workers so the food wouldn't go to waste. He didn't complain when I made pizza over and over to get it right, or when bags of bread dough tumbled out of the refrigerator unexpectedly, or when I sent him to the store for emergency rations of flour. I still don't know why he puts up with me, but I'm glad he does.

CONTENTS

INTRODUCTION

I can remember my fascination as a child, watching my mother knead bread . . .

Screeeeeeeeeech!

Let's back up a bit. To my recollection, my mother never baked any bread—or cakes or cookies or pies—during my childhood. She was a good cook, but rumor has it that after losing a pie-making contest to my father, she quit baking. That was a good decade or so before I was born, so I have no idea if her pie was even edible.

And she never baked anything from scratch again. That one failure stopped her in her tracks and she never attempted pie crust or bought yeast for bread. Heck, she didn't even bake boxed cake mixes. That was up to me and my Easy Bake® Oven.

The first whiff of home-baked bread I experienced was when Mom discovered frozen bread dough. I was enthralled at watching it rise, slowly and surely, until it peeked over the top of the loaf pan. Then it rose even more in the oven, like magic. The smell of baking bread was intoxicating. The crust was crisp and the interior was soft and fluffy. I had to know more.

It took quite a few more years before I baked my first loaf of bread completely from scratch, but the first one immediately led to a second one, and then a third. I stopped buying bread and I baked my own at least once a week.

It didn't take long before I abandoned recipes and started putting all sorts of things into the bread. First, it was different types of flour. Then it got crazy. What happens if you add peanut butter? Fruit purée? Marshmallows? It was an exciting adventure, and a delicious one.

This book is another stage of the adventure, and I'm happy to have you along with me.

GET READY TO BAKE BREAD!

MANY PEOPLE SAY THAT COOKING IS ART, but baking is science. I agree with that if they're talking about baking cakes or cookies or muffins. If we're making analogies about bread baking, I'd say it's more like live theater—with a stray cat loose in the building. The stray cat, of course, is the yeast. It can be unpredictable and hard to tame.

Professional bakeries turn out consistent products because they control every aspect of the baking process, from the source of the yeast to the protein content of the flour to the temperature of the water and the environmental temperature. At home, bakers don't have that consistency. It's hard enough to control room temperature to stay comfortable every day of the year, much less keep a consistent temperature for happy yeast.

Flour is another wild card, since brands vary in protein content, and moisture content can vary depending on humidity. And measuring flour by volume is inaccurate at best.

But none of that really matters. Bread is not a science experiment. It's art. It's live theater. It's a handmade product, and each loaf will be unique. That's the beauty of it.

Like good art, bread baking can take time, but unfortunately many people don't have half a day to devote to a loaf of bread. This book takes the process of bread making and fits it into a busy schedule by dividing the process into two or more parts. The bulk of the work—the kneading and forming—is done whenever the baker has time, whether that's after dinner, in early morning, or during the middle of the night. The dough is then refrigerated, where it rises slowly, developing flavor.

When the baker is ready, whether 8 hours later or even 24, the dough is ready to be baked.

To get the best results from this method, the first rise is important. The dough needs to double in volume, which means the yeast is energetic enough to accomplish a full second rise in the refrigerator.

In a cold house in winter, that might take a little longer than in a warm house in the summer, so bakers should take that into consideration. But as long as the yeast is alive, the bread will rise.

After that, it's all art. But every kind of art starts with supplies, equipment, and instructions. Read on to learn what you need to know to make breads of all kinds.

INGREDIENTS

BAKING SPRAY VS. COOKING SPRAY

For most of these recipes, I suggest using baking spray, which contains both oil and flour. While it's not strictly necessary, it's good insurance for making sure the loaves come out of the pans. Cooking spray doesn't include flour, so use it for gluten-free recipes. I suggest that you spend a little more and buy a name brand spray rather than a generic or store brand. A few of those cheaper brands left residue on my baking pans that was very difficult to wash off.

Instead of using spray, you can also oil the pans with a thin layer of your favorite cooking oil.

FLOUR

Flour is inconsistent at best. The weight of a cup of flour can vary dramatically depending on how it is put into the cup. But that's not the only issue. Protein levels vary wildly from brand to brand, and moisture content can vary depending on ambient humidity where the flour is stored. So even if flour is accurately weighed, its ability to absorb liquid can vary a lot, so the same ratio of liquid to flour can seem soft and sloppy for one baker, while it seems dense to another.

For bread flour, I like King Arthur Flour because it has a consistently high protein level. With other flour varieties like rye and whole wheat, there is even more variation from brand to brand and type to type. Use what's available in your area or what you like.

White rice flour is handy to have on hand. I use it a lot on top of rising bread dough that might stick to the plastic wrap that's covering it. The flour stays white during baking, so it makes a nice contrast against a dark crust, and it doesn't have an unpleasant raw taste.

Gluten-free mixes

You can buy any number of gluten-free flour blends at the grocery store and online, and they're particularly useful if you don't do a lot of gluten-free baking and don't want to make your own mix. The King Arthur gluten-free multipurpose flour was highly recommended by gluten-free friends, but several others were also mentioned.

SALT

Salt, like flour, varies in weight depending on type and brand. I use Morton's® kosher salt for all of my bread. If you use table salt, use slightly less than the recipes call for. If you use Diamond Crystal® salt, use slightly more. For the most part, salt is "to taste" so you can vary the amount based on what you like.

While there are a few saltless breads, I don't recommend leaving it out entirely, and it's not all about taste. Salt regulates the yeast, and a saltless bread can rise out of control—and then it's likely to collapse.

SWEETENERS

Most of my bread recipes include sugar. While it's not necessary for the yeast, which is perfectly happy to snack on the flour, it does help with browning, and a brown crust is a beautiful thing. If you like, you can substitute raw cane sugar, brown sugar, agave, or honey for the sugar in most recipes, keeping in mind that if you use a wet sweetener like agave, you might need to compensate by adding a little less water or a little more flour.

Honey is a special case, because some types are naturally antibacterial, and that property can sometimes affect yeast. When you open a new jar of honey, test it with your yeast. Add ½ teaspoon of honey to 1 cup of lukewarm water, then add a pinch of yeast. If the yeast doesn't bubble after about 5 minutes, you might want to consider a different brand of honey for bread making.

WATER

Many bread recipes call for warmer water, but I find that the biggest failure in bread baking is due to killing the yeast by using water that is too hot. Room temperature water is sufficient, and some of these recipes—notably the pastries—call for cold liquid, and the dough still rises.

YEAST

Most of the recipes in this book call for active dry yeast, since it has better staying power than instant yeast, which is formulated for a fast rise rather than a long, slow rise. In this case, brand matters. The active dry yeast made by Red Star is a smaller pellet size, similar to instant yeast, so it can be added directly to the dough mixture without needing to be softened first. If you're using a different brand of yeast, you should add it to the water and sugar and let it sit for about 5 minutes before proceeding with the kneading.

If you don't have any other yeast on hand, you can use an instant yeast, but the results might not be as great as they could be.

EGG WASH

If you want seeds or nuts to stick to the top of a loaf of bread, an egg wash is the best way to accomplish that. It's a simple mixture of 1 egg and a bit of water. You can also brush it onto any loaf when you want a shiny crust.

EQUIPMENT
DANISH DOUGH WHISK

If you're going to do a lot of dough-mixing by hand, a Danish dough whisk can come in handy. It's much easier and more efficient than trying to mix bread dough with a wooden spoon.

FOOD PROCESSOR

For the pastry recipes in particular, I use a food processor, but it's not strictly required. It just makes the job easier.

STAND MIXER

Strictly speaking, a stand mixer is not required, but it makes the job much easier, particularly if you're making multiple batches of dough in a day. Kneading by hand can be relaxing if you've got nothing else on the agenda, but on a busy day, it's nice to be able to throw all the ingredients into the stand mixer and let it knead while you attend to other things.

The great thing about a stand mixer is that it doesn't care if a dough is sticky, wet, dense, or buttery. When kneading by hand, there's a tendency to add more and more flour to keep dough from sticking to the work surface or hands, which can add a whole lot more flour to a recipe than is called for.

Meanwhile, doughs that start out dense and have butter added later can be hard to knead properly. And adding butter to a dough like that by hand can be frustrating.

PARCHMENT PAPER OR SILICONE MAT

I use a lot of parchment paper for baking because it makes cleanup so much easier, and there's less chance the dough will stick. I buy mine in bulk from a restaurant-supply house.

Silicone mats are also very useful, particularly when you're baking something that might be sticky, like a sugary bun or one with cheese that might ooze out.

BAKING PANS

One of my favorite baking pans is a 9 x 13-inch covered baking pan made by Good Cook. The cover is intended for storage of the baked goods or for transporting the goodies, but I use the cover when I'm letting shaped buns rise in the refrigerator. Because the cover is rigid, pans can be stacked on top of each other, and the lid sits up high enough to not interfere with the rising dough. I've also placed other pans inside that pan, like the 5 x 3-inch mini loaf pans, to keep them covered while dough is rising.

For doughs baked in a muffin pan, I have a similar covered pan.

PLASTIC WRAP OR BAGS

Dough needs to be covered during rising, and plastic wrap is handy, but you need to keep in mind that the dough needs room to expand. I actually prefer using large plastic bakery bags that I buy from King Arthur. I put the whole pan in the bag, leave plenty of air space, and clip the bag closed.

OVENS

You can add ovens to the list of unpredictable things. Most home ovens are not as precisely calibrated as we imagine, and the temperature inside fluctuates during

the baking cycle. This isn't something to stress over it's something to adjust to. Bread is accommodating, so a few degrees in either direction isn't critical. The one exception is the sweet doughs, and particularly those with sugary fillings that could burn. Those do need to be baked at a lower temperature so they have a chance to cook through before they burn.

INSTANT-READ THERMOMETER

I know some people get finicky about the exact temperature of the water or the prebaked dough or the butter, eggs, or oil. Considering how inexact everything else is, I can't get behind that extreme fussiness. The one place a thermometer is very useful is when testing to see whether a bread is fully baked or not, and it's

particularly useful when checking gluten-free loaves, since the margin for error there is much smaller.

METHODS
MEASURING

It's best to weigh flour on a kitchen scale, since flour can weigh anywhere from 4 to nearly 6 ounces per cup, depending on how it is weighed. No matter how you measure your flour, be sure to use a spoon to transfer flour from the bag to the cup measure. Scooping a cup into the flour might seem easier, but it compacts the flour and will significantly alter the weight. Other ingredients are fine measured by volume, since they don't vary nearly as much. For add-in ingredients like chopped nuts, seeds, or toppings, you can add more or less, to taste. It's wise to not stray too far from

recommended amounts, but a little more or less won't kill the recipe.

If you don't have a scale to weigh your flour (and sometimes depending on the brand and type of flour you use), you might need to add more flour or water to compensate for measuring differences.

MIXING

For most of the recipes in this book, all of the dough ingredients are mixed together at the same time. If you're using an active dry yeast brand other than Red Star, you should let the yeast soften in water before adding the rest of the ingredients.

For most recipes, mixing is the prelude to kneading, but there are a few recipes where the dough is mixed until well combined, then refrigerated. The key is to make sure there are no lumps of dry flour in the dough, but excessive mixing isn't required.

KNEADING

Most of the recipes in this book can be kneaded by machine or by hand. For a few recipes, machine kneading is highly recommended. As the dough is kneaded, you'll see it transform from a ragged-looking shaggy mess to something that is smooth (barring add-in ingredients) and elastic.

For hand kneading, every baker has his or her own favorite method. Work the dough in a way that feels comfortable and natural to you.

SHAPING

The goal when shaping dough is to get a good, tight skin on the outside of the loaf. But let's face it: that takes some practice. Sometimes a ragged-looking rough dough is more attractive than one that is perfectly shaped. If your loaves or buns aren't perfect, don't fret. Throw around the words "artisan" and "rustic" and no one will be the wiser.

Because the gluten in the dough relaxes during the resting time, the doughs tend to spread out. Depending on the other ingredients, some spread more than they rise, which is fine for some, but not so fine for others. The solution is to bake these breads in pans that contain their spread. That's why so many of these breads are baked in baking pans rather than left as free-form shapes on a baking sheet.

RISING

With this method, the first rise is the key. The dough should double in volume, whether that takes 50 minutes or an hour and 15 minutes. In a cold room in winter, it will take longer, so if you're shivering, find a warm spot to park your dough. The ideal temperature for that first rise is about 85°F, so if your environment is warmer or colder, be prepared for the dough to rise faster or slower in that first stage.

REFRIGERATION

This is the magical step in the process. The dough rises faster at first, but slows down as it chills. Eventually, the rise is nearly imperceptible, which is why the dough can be kept in the refrigerator for anywhere from 8 to 24 hours, and sometimes much longer. When the dough reaches refrigerator temperature, it's rising so slowly that it's unlikely to over-rise. The long, slow rise also improves the flavor and texture of the bread, compared to breads left at room temperature for the final rise before baking.

During refrigeration, the dough needs to be covered so it doesn't dry out. I love the lidded pans for that reason, and some of my pans fit into the large baking bags. Covering large baking pans can be problematic. Plastic wrap doesn't want to stick, and bags aren't big enough. My solution, as long as the dough won't be rising too high, is to use a second baking sheet flipped upside-down, as a cover. To hold it in place during refrigeration, I use rubber bands.

HEATING

When you bake cookies, have you noticed that the first batch is never the same as subsequent ones? That's because the oven signals that it's ready before it really is. The air temperature might be hot enough, but the temperature isn't really stabilized, so when you open that oven door, the hot air rushes out and it takes a while for the temperature to recover. Later, when the walls of the oven are hot, the temperature is much more stable.

I recommend heating the oven for 30 minutes before baking. This time also gives the dough time to recover a bit from the chill of the refrigerator. If your oven is already hot, you can bake directly from the refrigerator—the choice is yours.

On the other hand, if the dough looks like it needs a little more rising time, it's perfectly fine to leave the dough at room temperature even longer.

NO SLASHING REQUIRED

Because of the way the refrigerated dough rises, there's no need to slash the top of the dough. But if you want to make slashes for decorative purposes, that's your choice. On some breads, the slashes might not widen very much in the oven, or they might heal themselves and leave very little of your art.

DONENESS OF BREAD

Ovens are not well-calibrated, and it's also hard to know precisely how cold your refrigerator is, so baking times are never going to be exact. The breads should all have a nicely browned crust, but a more reliable gauge is temperature. Make sure you're checking the temperature near the center of the loaf (using an instant-read thermometer), and make sure you're testing the dough temperature and not any filling ingredients. Most breads will not come to any great harm if they're slightly overcooked, but it's best not to go too far over, if you can help it.

Sweet and enriched breads are done when they reach 190° to 195°F; standard white loaves are done at 195° to 200°F; gluten-free bread's optimum temperature is 206°F; whole grain and rye loaves need to cook to 205° to 210°F.

MAKING A SOURDOUGH STARTER

A sourdough starter is a simple concept—let some flour and water hang around for a while and almost magically, the correct combination of yeast and bacteria will take up residence. And that same combination, when healthy and happy, creates an environment that's unfriendly to unwanted organisms.

Sourdough starter takes between 6 and 12 days before it's ready to use. You'll know it's ready when you see that it bubbles furiously and rises in the jar within an hour or so of feeding. This could happen on Day 5 or Day 12.

There's not a lot of preplanning required. All you really need is some sort of reasonable containment vessel, like a canning jar with a lid (you won't use the lid while you're growing the starter, but you'll use it when you store it), some flour, some water, and something to stir your mixture. A scale is nice if you want to be precise, or you can use volume measures or just eyeball it as best you can.

I use plain tap water for starters, fresh from the faucet. If your water is highly chlorinated, you might want to let the water sit overnight so the chlorine dissipates. If your water is otherwise nasty tasting, it doesn't necessarily mean it will be bad for sourdough, although it might be. If you're worried, buy a bottle of water.

(handwritten margin note: IN VANCOUVER IT IS)

DAY 1

My goal in creating a sourdough starter was to come up with a method that would be easy for anyone. I also didn't want to end up with an excess of starter that would have to be thrown away, so I started with a very small amount. I find that starters seem to work better if they're very wet at the beginning, so I started by combining ½ ounce of flour and 1 ounce of water. That's all.

Cover the jar with plastic wrap and store on the kitchen counter. Do not refrigerate. Forget about it until the next day.

While your just-started starter sits, the enzymes in the flour get to work, and some of the starch in the flour starts converting to sugar. Soon wild yeasts arrive and a new sourdough starter is born.

DAY 2

Many sourdough starter recipes require a lot of feeding, but stirring is just as important as feeding—maybe more so. Stir the mixture whenever you think about it. You don't need to stir on schedule, but whenever it's convenient give the mixture a little stir, whether it's a couple times a day or a dozen because you happen to be in the kitchen.

DAY 3

Feed the starter with 1 ounce each of flour and water. Stir as on Day 2.

DAY 4

Feed the starter with 1 ounce of flour and ½ ounce of water. Stir as before. Now there is an equal weight of flour and water in the jar, and this is the ratio we'll keep throughout the process.

DAYS 5 TO 12

From now on, it's all about feeding once a day and stirring whenever you think about it. Unlike some starter recipes that require each feeding to double the existing amount of starter, I feed the same amount each day. Just add 1 ounce each of flour and water.

As mentioned, the starter is ready to use when you see that it bubbles furiously and rises in the jar within an hour or so of feeding. It should actually double in volume. This could happen on Day 5 or it could happen on Day 12—each starter is unique.

If your starter isn't bubbling vigorously after 2 weeks, dump out all but about ¼ inch of starter in the jar. You can add that discarded starter to another dough to add flavor, if you like, or use it in pancakes or waffles.

To invigorate that remaining starter, feed it three times a day, doubling the amount each time. In about 2 days, you should have a very lively starter. If not, then you might want to try again, perhaps using a different brand of flour or using bottled water rather than tap water.

You can also purchase starters online, if you have no luck trapping local yeasts.

STORING YOUR STARTER

Before you store your starter, feed it. Then cover the jar and stash it in the refrigerator.

People often worry that they've killed their starter by leaving it in the refrigerator for a long time without feeding it. But when starter is refrigerated, the yeasts slow down and become practically dormant.

A yellowish liquid usually forms on top, referred to as "hootch" by sourdough folks. Hootch isn't a big deal. Sometimes the hootch starts looking like it's got black sediment in it, which is just yeast cells that have died off. This isn't a big deal either, and chances are there are plenty more yeast cells still alive. Some people stir the hootch back into the starter before they feed it, and some people discard it. Either is fine.

It's a good idea to feed your refrigerated sourdough starter occasionally, even though it's mostly dormant. Once a month is sufficient, although I've left mine for as long as 6 months and brought it back to life.

LOAF BREADS

RUSTIC SOURDOUGH BREAD

The gluten in dough that rests overnight relaxes the dough, so bread tends to spread during baking. This sourdough is no exception, except that the sides of the cake pan support the bread, letting it rise higher rather than spreading.

The great thing about sourdoughs is that no two starters will ever be alike, and even the same starter will change over time. The way you treat your starter also affects the flavor. A well-fed and well-cared-for starter will be mild, while a starter that missed a feeding or two is likely to be more sour. (For more on sourdough starter, see pp. 9–10.)

Like starters, sourdough breads are different from each other. Some rise fast, some slow; some brown more than others. Once you've baked with your starter a few times, you'll get to know its quirks and characteristics and its effects on this recipe. If you don't want to make your own starter, buy it in dried form online.

MAKES ONE 8-INCH ROUND LOAF

4 ounces (by weight) sourdough starter

4 cups (18 ounces) bread flour, divided

1¼ cups room temperature water, divided

1 teaspoon kosher salt

Nonstick baking spray

Cornmeal, for the pan

TIP

You can also bake this bread in a 9 x 5-inch loaf pan.

ON PREP DAY 1

Combine the sourdough starter, 1 cup flour, and ½ cup water in a stand mixer or a large bowl. Cover and let the mixture sit overnight at room temperature.

ON PREP DAY 2

1. Add the remaining ¾ cup water, remaining 3 cups flour, and the salt to the bowl containing the sourdough starter mixture. Knead with the dough hook of the stand mixer or mix by hand until the dough becomes smooth. The dough will be wet and sticky, but don't be tempted to add more flour.

2. Spray an 8-inch round cake pan with baking spray and sprinkle cornmeal in the bottom of the pan.

3. Form the dough into a ball and place it in the center of the cake pan. Cover the pan loosely with plastic wrap—you need to leave space for the dough to rise—or place the whole pan in a large plastic bag and tie the open end shut. Refrigerate the bread overnight or up to 24 hours before baking.

ON BAKING DAY

1. Remove the pan from the refrigerator and heat the oven to 350°F.

2. Remove the plastic from the pan and bake the bread until it is deep brown and the internal temperature reaches 195°F on an instant-read thermometer, about 65 minutes. Cool completely on a wire rack before slicing.

BACON, TOMATO, *and* CHEDDAR LOAF

All the flavors of a BLT, plus the extra savory touch of some Cheddar—what's not to love? Vary the size of the chopped tomatoes and cheese based on your preference for smaller bits scattered throughout the bread or larger pieces appearing here and there.

The bacon is best if it's cooked until very crisp and crumbly; less well-done bacon tends to be chewy in the bread.

MAKES ONE 9 X 5-INCH LOAF

ON PREP DAY

1. Combine all of the ingredients and knead by hand (mix first in a large bowl, then turn out and knead) or in a stand mixer fitted with the dough hook, until the dough is elastic. It will be lumpy, of course, but the dough itself should be stretchy.

2. Cover the bowl with plastic wrap and let the dough rise until it has doubled in size, about 1 hour in a warm room.

3. Meanwhile, spray a 9 x 5-inch loaf pan with baking spray.

4. Turn the dough out onto a lightly floured surface and pat it into a rough 8-inch square. Fold the top half to about the middle of the dough and press the edge down to secure it. Fold the top over again, this time to within about an inch or so of the bottom. Press the edge to seal. Now grab the bottom of the dough and pull it up to meet the dough roll you've created and seal the seam. Pinch the ends closed and place the dough, seam side down, in the prepared loaf pan.

5. Cover the pan with plastic wrap or place the whole pan in a large plastic bag and tie the open end shut. Refrigerate the dough overnight or up to 24 hours before baking. The dough should be fully risen after about 6 hours, but a longer rest is good for it.

ON BAKING DAY

1. Take the pan out of the refrigerator and heat the oven to 350°F. Put a rack in the center of the oven.

2. Remove the plastic and bake the bread until it is richly browned and the internal temperature reaches 195°F on an instant-read thermometer, about 55 minutes. Transfer the bread from the pan and cool completely on a wire rack before slicing.

1½ cups room temperature water

2¼ teaspoons active dry yeast

1 tablespoon sugar

3 cups (13½ ounces) bread flour, plus more as needed

½ cup (3 ounces) semolina flour

3 ounces sun-dried tomatoes, chopped

4 ounces Cheddar, diced

6 strips bacon, cooked (1 tablespoon fat reserved) and chopped or crumbled

½ teaspoon kosher salt

Nonstick baking spray

TIP

If you'd rather, form the dough into a round and place on a baking sheet. Cover with plastic wrap to let fully rise and bake following the recipe instructions.

OATMEAL-HONEY-DATE LOAF

While this makes a great breakfast bread, it's also perfect for sandwiches. The sweet dates accent the savory flavor without overwhelming it.

You can use either quick-cooking oats or old-fashioned rolled oats for this loaf. The quick-cooking oats will dissolve more into the bread while the old-fashioned oats will be visible and add little bits of a pleasant chew.

A little bit of rye flour adds to the savory flavor of the bread. If you don't have white rye flour, you can use a light rye.

MAKES ONE 9 X 5-INCH LOAF

1 cup rolled oats
$\frac{1}{2}$ cup ($2\frac{1}{2}$ ounces) white rye flour
$2\frac{1}{2}$ cups ($11\frac{1}{4}$ ounces) bread flour, plus more as needed
2 tablespoons honey
$1\frac{1}{4}$ cups room temperature water
1 teaspoon kosher salt
2 tablespoons olive oil
$2\frac{1}{4}$ teaspoons active dry yeast
$\frac{1}{2}$ cup chopped dates
Nonstick baking spray

ON PREP DAY

1. Combine all of the ingredients and knead by hand (mix first in a large bowl, then turn out and knead) or in a stand mixer fitted with the dough hook, until the dough is elastic. It will be lumpy, of course, but the dough itself should be stretchy.

2. Cover the bowl with plastic wrap and let the dough rise until it has doubled in size, about 1 hour in a warm room.

3. Meanwhile, spray a 9 x 5-inch loaf pan with baking spray.

4. Turn the dough out onto a lightly floured surface and pat it into a rough 8-inch square. Fold the top half to about the middle of the dough and press the edge down to secure it. Fold the top over again, this time to within about an inch or so of the bottom. Press the edge to seal. Now pull the bottom of the dough up to meet the dough roll you've created and seal the seam. Pinch the ends closed and place the dough, seam side down, in the prepared loaf pan.

5. Cover the pan with plastic wrap or place the whole pan in a large plastic bag and tie the open end shut. Refrigerate overnight or up to 24 hours before baking. The dough should be fully risen after about 6 hours, but a longer rest is good for it.

ON BAKING DAY

1. Take the pan out of the refrigerator and heat the oven to 350°F.

2. Remove the plastic and bake the bread until it is richly browned and the internal temperature reaches 195°F on an instant-read thermometer, about 55 minutes. Remove the bread from the pan and cool completely on a rack before slicing.

Oatmeal-Honey-Date Loaf with Cinnamon-Sugar Compound Butter
(recipe on p. 179)

LIGHT and DARK MARBLE RYE

Marble rye used to fascinate me when I was a kid—I loved the swirl of different colors and I'd try to eat one swirl at a time. It never worked, but it was fun trying.

Most marble rye breads have a broad swirl, but this one has a rather tight spiral with thin layers of the dark and light ryes. This bread uses white rye flour and pumpernickel flour for the greatest difference in color. Seek out white rye flour, even if you have to buy it online. Of course, you can still make this bread using light rye, which is more likely to be available at your grocery store, but you won't get the variance of color.

If you can't find pumpernickel flour, dark rye will work just fine. The cocoa powder added to the dough will get the dark swirl dark enough to make a difference, but you don't actually taste the chocolate.

MAKES ONE 9 X 5-INCH LOAF

ON PREP DAY 1

Make the base dough: Combine the water, yeast, and bread flour in a medium bowl. Stir well to combine. Cover the bowl with plastic wrap and let it rest on your counter at room temperature overnight or up to 24 hours.

ON PREP DAY 2

1. Split the base dough in half and transfer half to another bowl (or the bowl of your stand mixer). Try to get the halves as close to equal as possible.

2. To one half, add the light rye ingredients: white rye flour, salt, sugar, and olive oil. Mix to combine, then turn out and knead by hand or in your stand mixer fitted with the dough hook until the dough is smooth and elastic.

3. Set that dough aside, covered with plastic wrap, while you work with the second half of the base dough. To that, add the dark rye ingredients: pumpernickel flour, salt, sugar, cocoa powder, and olive oil. Mix and knead as you did for the first half.

continued

FOR THE BASE DOUGH

1½ cups room temperature water

1 teaspoon active dry yeast

2 cups (9 ounces) bread flour, plus more as needed

FOR THE LIGHT RYE DOUGH

1 cup (4½ ounces) white rye flour

½ teaspoon kosher salt

1 teaspoon sugar

1 tablespoon olive oil

FOR THE DARK RYE DOUGH

1 cup (4½ ounces) pumpernickel flour

½ teaspoon kosher salt

1 teaspoon sugar

1 tablespoon cocoa powder

1 tablespoon olive oil

Nonstick baking spray

Light and Dark Marble Rye with Chunky Apple and Cinnamon Spread
(*recipe on p. 180*)

4. Now, check the density of the two doughs by poking them to get a feel for the dough—they should be about the same (one shouldn't feel like modeling clay and the other like a sofa cushion). You don't want one very wet and the other very dry. The cocoa powder will affect the texture of the dark dough, but otherwise they should feel evenly dense. If one dough feels much softer and squishier than the other, knead in a little extra flour. You shouldn't need more than a tablespoon, if any at all.

5. Place the two doughs in separate large bowls, cover, and allow them to rest at room temperature for 30 minutes. Meanwhile, spray a 9 x 5-inch loaf pan with baking spray.

6. When the doughs have rested, flour your work surface lightly (with any flour other than the pumpernickel flour). Roll out each dough to a 6-inch square.

7. Place the dark dough on top of the light dough and roll them out to approximately 10 x 16 inches. Starting at one of the short ends, roll the doughs together, jellyroll style, and seal the seam. Pinch the ends closed and place the roll, seam side down, in the prepared loaf pan.

8. Cover the pan with plastic wrap or place the whole pan in a large plastic bag and tie the end closed. Refrigerate overnight.

ON BAKING DAY

1. Take the pan out of the refrigerator and heat the oven to 350°F.

2. Remove the plastic and bake the loaf until it is nicely browned and the interior temperature reaches 205°F on an instant-read thermometer, about 50 minutes. Remove the bread from the pan and cool completely on a rack before slicing.

RICH EGG *and* BUTTER LOAF

This bread makes great sandwiches and wonderful French toast, and it's lovely toasted with a small smear of peanut butter or stone fruit jam.

The icing on the cake, so to speak, is the egg wash that gives the bread a shiny surface and helps it brown to a lovely mahogany color. You can leave off the egg wash—the bread will still be fine.

This recipe calls for room temperature butter, but the truth is that if you're kneading with a machine (see the tip on p. 22), you can add butter that's still chilly—the stand mixer will be able to knead it in without a problem. Just cut it into tablespoon-size pieces.

MAKES ONE 9 X 5-INCH LOAF

3 cups (13$\frac{1}{2}$ ounces) bread flour, plus more as needed

2$\frac{1}{4}$ teaspoons active dry yeast

$\frac{1}{2}$ cup room temperature water

$\frac{1}{4}$ cup heavy cream

2 eggs

1 tablespoon sugar

1 teaspoon kosher salt

8 tablespoons unsalted butter, at room temperature

Nonstick baking spray

Egg wash (1 egg mixed with 1 tablespoon water; optional)

ON PREP DAY

1. Combine the flour, yeast, water, heavy cream, eggs, and sugar in a stand mixer fitted with the dough hook and knead until the dough is smooth.

2. Add the salt and butter, 1 tablespoon at a time, kneading until the butter is incorporated each time.

3. Cover the bowl with plastic wrap and let the dough rise until it has doubled in size, about 1 hour in a warm room.

4. Meanwhile, spray a 9 x 5-inch loaf pan with baking spray.

5. Turn the dough out onto a lightly floured surface and pat it into a rough 8-inch square. Fold the top half to about the middle of the dough and press the edge down to secure it. Fold the top over again, this time to within about an inch or so of the bottom. Press the edge to seal. Now pull the bottom of the dough up to meet the dough roll you've created and seal the seam. Pinch the ends closed and place the dough, seam side down, in the prepared loaf pan.

6. Cover the pan with plastic wrap or place the whole pan in a large plastic bag and tie the open end shut. Refrigerate overnight or up to 24 hours before baking. The dough should be fully risen after about 6 hours, but a longer rest is good for it.

continued

ON BAKING DAY

1. Take the pan out of the refrigerator and heat the oven to 350°F.

2. Remove the plastic and brush the top of the dough with the egg wash, if using. Bake the bread until it is richly browned and the internal temperature reaches 190°F on an instant-read thermometer, about 50 minutes. Remove the bread from the pan and cool completely on a rack before slicing.

TIP

Because of the large amount of butter in this bread, it needs to be added at the end of kneading or it would difficult for the gluten to form properly. Adding butter to dough when you're kneading by hand can be messy. It can be done, but I highly recommend using a stand mixer to do the work for you.

Rich Egg and Butter Loaf with Stone Fruit and Almond Jam
(recipe on p. 192)

SOURDOUGH RYE BREAD

While I love all sorts of sourdoughs, I particularly like sourdough rye—the tang of the sourdough is perfect with the flavor of the rye flour. Choose your favorite rye flour for this recipe—the sourdough will make it shine.

The dough is very wet and sticky and can be hard to knead by hand, so use a stand mixer if you have one. There's a temptation to add more flour to eliminate the stickiness, but don't do it—you'll risk adding too much.

MAKES ONE 9 X 5-INCH LOAF

ON PREP DAY 1

Combine the sourdough starter, rye flour, and ½ cup water in a stand mixer or in a large bowl. Cover and let the mixture sit overnight at room temperature.

ON PREP DAY 2

1. Add the remaining ¾ cup water, the bread flour, salt, and olive oil to the bowl containing the sourdough starter mixture. Knead with the dough hook of the stand mixer or mix by hand until the dough becomes smooth. The dough will be wet and sticky, but don't be tempted to add more flour.

2. Spray a 9 x 5-inch loaf pan with baking spray and transfer the dough to the pan. With lightly greased fingertips, spread the dough in the pan to even it out.

3. Cover the pan with plastic wrap or place the whole pan in a large plastic bag and tie the open end shut. Refrigerate the bread overnight or up to 24 hours before baking.

ON BAKING DAY

1. Remove the pan from the refrigerator and heat the oven to 350°F.

2. Remove the plastic and bake the bread until it is deep brown and the internal temperature reaches 195°F on an instant-read thermometer, about 55 minutes. Cool completely on a wire rack before slicing.

4 ounces (by weight)
   sourdough starter
1 cup (4½ ounces) rye flour
1¼ cups room temperature
   water, divided
2½ cups (11¼ ounces)
   bread flour, divided
1 teaspoon kosher salt
1 tablespoon olive oil
Nonstick baking spray

TIP

If you plan on making a lot of sourdough rye, put a few tablespoons of starter in a new jar and begin feeding it with rye flour in the same way you feed your white flour starter.

BAGUETTES

These aren't traditional baguettes, but they're darned good impostors. Slather them with butter, serve them with pasta, or use them to make garlic bread or a sub sandwich. They'll stand up to those tasks proudly.

This bread requires your attention three times over a 3-day span—once to mix the dough, once to form the loaves, and once to bake—but none of those steps takes much time at all. You'll find this bread well worth the waiting time.

Be sure to use the rice flour for dusting the bread. It's like the Teflon® of the food world: It will keep the dough from sticking to the plastic wrap, and it stays white during baking, which gives the bread an interesting appearance.

MAKES TWO 12-INCH-LONG BAGUETTES

1¼ cups room temperature water

2¼ teaspoons active dry yeast

3 cups (13½ ounces) bread flour, plus more as needed

1 tablespoon sugar

1 teaspoon kosher salt

1 teaspoon olive oil (for coating the bag)

Rice flour (for dusting the loaves)

ON PREP DAY 1

1. Combine all of the ingredients except the oil and rice flour and knead by hand (mix first in a large bowl, then turn out and knead) or in a stand mixer fitted with the dough hook, until the dough is well combined and a little less shaggy. You don't want it to become elastic, but it should be well-mixed and coherent.

2. Drizzle the olive oil into a gallon-size zip-top plastic bag and transfer the dough to the bag. (Flour your hands first, as the dough is sticky.) Squish the dough around in the bag to coat it with the olive oil. Even though the dough is quite sticky, the oil will come between it and the plastic bag as you give it a gentle massage.

3. Squeeze the air out of the bag, seal, and refrigerate at least overnight. This dough improves with age, so you can leave it in the refrigerator an extra day, if you like.

ON PREP DAY 2

1. Line a half-sheet baking pan with parchment paper.

2. Flour your work surface lightly and turn out the dough. Divide it in half, and form each half into a log about 13 inches long. You can do this by rolling the dough like a kid making a snake out of clay, or you can press and stretch each piece of dough to about 12 inches long, then fold the edges of the long sides together and pinch to seal the seams.

3. Place the two logs on the parchment-lined baking sheet, leaving about 2 inches of space between them for rising. Dust the tops of the loaves with rice flour and cover the pan with plastic wrap or place the whole pan in a large plastic bag and tie the end closed. Refrigerate the loaves overnight.

ON BAKING DAY

1. Take the pan out of the refrigerator and heat the oven to 350°F. The loaves might have flattened a bit and spread, but that's to be expected. They will rise as they bake.

2. Remove the plastic and bake the loaves until they are medium golden-brown and the internal temperature reaches 195°F on an instant-read thermometer, about 35 minutes. Transfer the loaves to a rack and cool completely before slicing.

Baguettes with Wine Jam
(*recipe on p. 193*)

MINI SUNFLOWER SEED LOAVES

Sunflower seeds add a wonderful texture to bread—they're not as hard or crunchy as nuts, but they add a flavor reminiscent of nuts. The seeds also add an interesting bumpy texture to the crust of the bread where they appear close to the surface. If you like, you can brush the loaf with an egg wash and add even more seeds to the top of the loaf, where they'll get just a bit toasty.

These mini loaves make lovely hostess gifts and are perfect on the breakfast or brunch table, too.

MAKES FOUR 5¾ X 3-INCH LOAVES

ON PREP DAY

1. Combine all of the ingredients except the egg wash and a reserved ¼ cup of sunflower seeds and knead by hand (mix first in a large bowl, then turn out and knead) or in a stand mixer fitted with the dough hook, until the dough is elastic.

2. Cover the bowl with plastic wrap and let the dough rise until it has doubled in size, about 1 hour in a warm room.

3. Meanwhile, spray four mini loaf pans (5¾ x 3 inches) with baking spray.

4. Turn the dough out onto a lightly floured surface and divide it into 4 equal portions. Working with one at a time, pat it into a rough 5-inch square, then roll the dough, jellyroll style, to form a fat log. Pinch the seam and ends closed and place the log, seam side down, into one of the prepared pans. Continue with the other three pieces of dough.

5. Cover the pans with plastic wrap or place them on a baking sheet (for easier handling) and put the whole pan in a large plastic bag and tie the open end shut. Refrigerate overnight or up to 24 hours before baking.

ON BAKING DAY

1. Take the pans out of the refrigerator and heat the oven to 350°F.

2. Remove the plastic, brush the breads with the egg wash, and sprinkle the reserved ¼ cup of sunflower seeds onto the top. For easier handling, you can leave the mini pans on the baking sheet or remove them and place directly on the oven rack. Bake the breads until they are nicely browned and the internal temperature reaches 195°F on an instant-read thermometer, about 25 minutes. Remove the breads from the pans and cool completely on a rack before slicing.

1¼ cups room temperature water

2¼ teaspoons active dry yeast

1 tablespoon sugar

2½ cups (11¼ ounces) bread flour, plus more as needed

½ cup (3 ounces) semolina flour

1 teaspoon kosher salt

1 tablespoon olive oil

¾ cup sunflower seeds, divided

Nonstick baking spray

Egg wash (1 egg beaten with 1 tablespoon water)

WHITE, WHOLE WHEAT, *and* RYE BRAID

Braided breads are pretty, but unless you're making just one type of dough and braiding it, many recipes require making a full recipe of each type of dough. This recipe makes just one loaf of braided bread.

The vital wheat gluten in the rye dough helps give it a little more structure, but if you don't have it on hand, don't fret. It's there for insurance, but you can leave it out if you have to. If you do leave out the gluten, you'll need slightly less water, so cut back to just $1/2$ cup.

MAKES 1 LOAF APPROXIMATELY 14 INCHES LONG

ON PREP DAY

1. For all three doughs, the instructions are the same: mix all ingredients until combined (in a medium bowl or in the bowl of your stand mixer), then knead by hand or in a stand mixer fitted with the dough hook until the dough is elastic. I suggest starting with the rye dough, then the wheat, then the white. (The rye rises a bit more slowly, so it's good to give it a head start; white rises most quickly.)

2. After each dough is prepared, place it in a medium bowl, cover, and set aside in a warm place. When you've finished preparing the third dough, set a timer for 45 minutes and let all of the doughs rise.

3. Line a baking sheet with parchment paper.

4. When the doughs have risen, flour your work surface lightly. One at a time, turn out each dough and form it into a rope (as a child would roll a snake from clay) about 20 inches long.

5. Line up the three pieces of dough next to each other. Pinch the three together at one end, then braid them loosely. When you finish, pinch the ends together. Transfer the dough to the parchment-lined baking sheet. I like to arrange it diagonally on the sheet for more space. Tuck the pinched ends under to hide them, and straighten and arrange the dough so it's even. Cover with plastic wrap and refrigerate overnight or up to 24 hours.

ON BAKING DAY

1. Remove the baking sheet from the refrigerator and heat the oven to 350°F.

2. Remove the plastic and bake the bread until it is nicely browned and the internal temperature reaches 205°F on an instant-read thermometer, about 25 minutes. Transfer the loaf on parchment to a rack and let it cool completely before slicing.

FOR THE RYE DOUGH

- $1/2$ cup plus 1 tablespoon room temperature water
- 1 teaspoon active dry yeast
- 1 teaspoon sugar
- $3/4$ cup ($3\,3/8$ ounces) bread flour
- $1/2$ cup ($2\,1/2$ ounces) dark rye flour
- $1/2$ teaspoon kosher salt
- 1 teaspoon vital wheat gluten
- 1 teaspoon cocoa powder
- 2 teaspoons unsalted butter, at room temperature

FOR THE WHOLE WHEAT DOUGH

- 1 egg plus room temperature water to equal $1/2$ cup
- 1 teaspoon active dry yeast
- 1 teaspoon sugar
- $3/4$ cup ($3\,3/8$ ounces) bread flour
- $1/2$ cup ($2\,1/4$ ounces) whole wheat flour
- $1/2$ teaspoon kosher salt
- 1 teaspoon unsalted butter, at room temperature

FOR THE WHITE DOUGH

- $1/2$ cup room temperature water
- 1 teaspoon active dry yeast
- 1 teaspoon sugar
- $1\,1/4$ cups ($5\,5/8$ ounces) bread flour, plus more as needed
- $1/2$ teaspoon kosher salt
- 1 teaspoon olive oil

FRESH CORN *and* CHEDDAR LOAF

Fresh corn adds a pleasant sweetness and texture to this bread, and the Cheddar adds extra savory flavor. This makes a great sandwich bread. Use leftovers in any of the savory stratas in the Leftover chapter (see p. 164).

Because of the corn, store the bread in the refrigerator rather than at room temperature.

MAKES ONE 9 X 5-INCH LOAF

ON PREP DAY

1. Combine the water, yeast, sugar, flour, salt, and butter and knead by hand (mix first in a large bowl, then turn out and knead) or in a stand mixer fitted with the dough hook until smooth. The dough will be fairly stiff at this point.

2. Add the cheese and corn and continue kneading just until they are incorporated. At first, the dough will seem wet and sloppy from the moisture in the corn, but as the corn becomes incorporated, the dough will become softer and cohesive.

3. Cover the bowl and set aside to rise until the dough has doubled in size, about 1 hour in a warm room.

4. Spray a 9 x 5-inch loaf pan with baking spray.

5. Turn the dough out onto a lightly floured surface and pat it into a rough 8-inch square. Fold the top half to about the middle of the dough and press the edge down to secure it. Fold the top over again, this time to within about an inch or so of the bottom. Press the edge to seal. Now pull the bottom of the dough up to meet the dough roll you've created and seal the seam. Pinch the ends closed and place the dough, seam side down, in the prepared loaf pan.

6. Cover the pan with plastic wrap or place the whole pan in a large plastic bag and tie the open end shut. Refrigerate overnight or up to 24 hours before baking. The dough should be fully risen after about 6 hours.

ON BAKING DAY

1. Take the pan out of the refrigerator and heat the oven to 350°F.

2. Remove the plastic and bake the loaf until it is nicely browned and the internal temperature reaches 195°F on an instant-read thermometer, about 55 minutes. Remove the bread from the pan and cool completely on a rack before slicing.

1 cup room temperature water

2 1/4 teaspoons active dry yeast

1 tablespoon sugar

3 cups (13 1/2 ounces) bread flour, plus more as needed

1 teaspoon kosher salt

2 tablespoons unsalted butter

4 ounces shredded mild Cheddar

1 cup fresh corn kernels, roughly chopped into smaller pieces

Nonstick baking spray

TIP

When fresh corn isn't in season, substitute with frozen corn. In a pinch, you can use canned corn, but cut back a little on the salt.

GLUTEN-FREE SEED *and* NUT BREAD

I had many offers of help from folks in the gluten-free community when I mentioned on my blog that I wanted to make some of the recipes in this book gluten-free.

Elizabeth Barbone, author of *How to Cook Gluten-Free* and *Easy Gluten-Free Baking* was one of the first to volunteer. Elizabeth and I "met" online when we were both writing baking columns for *Serious Eats*. Hers were gluten-free and mine, of course, were gluten-filled.

The foundation for this loaf is one of Elizabeth's basic recipes, but I added seeds and nuts to give the loaf more texture and flavor. Even gluten eaters will like it.

MAKES ONE 9 X 5-INCH LOAF

ON PREP DAY

1. Spray a 9 x 5-inch loaf pan with cooking spray (don't use baking spray, which contains flour). Or brush the pan with cooking oil, if you prefer.

2. Combine all the ingredients in a stand mixer fitted with the paddle attachment. You can also mix this in a large bowl with a hand mixer. Beat for 5 minutes. The texture won't be like bread dough, but you will see the dough begin to seem a little gluey—like mashed potatoes that have gone wrong.

3. Transfer the dough to the prepared pan and smooth out the top with moistened fingers. Cover the pan with plastic wrap or place the pan in a large plastic bag and tie the open end shut. Refrigerate the dough overnight or up to 24 hours.

ON BAKING DAY

1. Take the pan out of the refrigerator and heat the oven to 350°F.

2. Remove the plastic from the pan. If you like, sprinkle the top with additional sesame seeds. Bake the loaf until it is nicely browned and the internal temperature reaches 205°F on an instant-read thermometer, about 1 hour 10 minutes. Turn out the bread onto a rack. Cool completely before slicing.

Nonstick cooking spray

2 1/2 cups (13 3/4 ounces) King Arthur Flour gluten-free multipurpose flour

1/2 cup nonfat dry milk

2 1/4 teaspoons active dry yeast

1 teaspoon kosher salt

1/4 cup cornstarch

1 tablespoon xanthan gum

1/4 cup chopped walnuts

1/4 cup sunflower seeds

1/4 cup flax seeds

1/4 cup sesame seeds, plus more for the top of the bread (optional)

3 eggs

1 1/2 cups room temperature water

2 tablespoons unsalted butter, at room temperature

TIP

Gluten-free breads tend to get stale—and moldy—much faster than standard bread. If you're not going to devour this immediately, freeze it.

SAUERKRAUT RYE

This is a moist dough due to the addition of the sauerkraut, which also adds a nice tang to the bread. Make sure you let this bread cool completely before slicing—it will be gummy if you slice it before it cools.

The amount of water you'll need depends on how well you drained the sauerkraut. You won't need more than 1 cup, but you might need less.

MAKES ONE 8 X 4-INCH LOAF

ON PREP DAY

1. Place the sauerkraut in a food processor and pulse several times to break the pieces into smaller bits.

2. Add the yeast, sugar, rye flour, and bread flour to the food processor, and pulse several times until everything is well combined.

3. With the food processor running, add the water as fast as the flour can absorb it. Start with only ¾ cup and add more, 1 tablespoon at a time, if needed. When the dough begins to gather together, add the caraway seeds and continue processing until the seeds are mostly incorporated into the dough.

4. Drizzle the olive oil into a bowl. Remove the dough from the food processor, form it into a ball, and place it in the bowl, turning to coat all sides of the dough with oil. Cover the bowl with plastic wrap and set aside in a warm place to rise until doubled, about 1 hour.

5. Spray an 8 x 4-inch loaf pan with baking spray or cooking oil spray, then sprinkle it generously with cornmeal.

6. When the dough has risen, flour your work surface and turn out the dough. Knead it just enough to knock out the air, then form it into a log about 8 inches long. Place the dough in the prepared pan. Sprinkle some flour on top of the dough (this will keep the dough from sticking to the plastic), and cover the pan with plastic wrap or slide it into a plastic bag and tie it closed. Place the pan in the refrigerator overnight or up to 24 hours.

1 cup well-drained, packed sauerkraut

1 teaspoon instant yeast

1 tablespoon sugar

1 cup (4½ ounces) rye flour

2 cups (9 ounces) bread flour, plus more as needed

¾ to 1 cup room temperature water

1 tablespoon caraway seeds

1 tablespoon olive oil

Nonstick baking spray or cooking oil spray

Cornmeal, for the pan

ON BAKING DAY

1. When you're ready to bake, heat the oven to 325°F. Remove the pan from the refrigerator. The dough is ready to bake when it has risen 1 inch over the top of the pan. If it has risen that much in the refrigerator, you can bake immediately. Otherwise, let the dough continue rising at room temperature until it has risen to the intended height.

2. Remove the plastic, slash the top of the dough as desired (I like to cut a horizontal gash down the center), and bake the bread until it is browned and the internal temperature reaches 205°F on an instant-read thermometer. Depending on how cold the dough was when you put it in the oven, this will be between 35 and 45 minutes. Turn the bread out of the pan and let it cool completely on a rack before slicing.

Sauerkraut Rye with Chive Cream Cheese
(recipe on p. 181)

SAVORY MONKEY BREAD

Monkey bread is usually sweet, but it can also be savory. The best thing about monkey bread is that it's fun to pull apart and there's no need to worry about the pieces being the same size. I purposely make some smaller and some larger, so there's an interesting variety. And they don't all have to be round—you can stretch some into longer shapes to add a little more interest.

This bread pairs well with Italian dishes, but it's great with just about anything, even just a little dab of butter.

Although this is meant to be a pull-apart loaf, you can also slice it, and you'll see the seedy seams running through the slices.

MAKES ONE 8-INCH SQUARE OR ROUND BREAD

ON PREP DAY

1. Combine all of the ingredients (except the seeds) and knead by hand (mix first in a large bowl, then turn out and knead) or in a stand mixer fitted with the dough hook, until the dough is elastic.

2. Cover the bowl with plastic wrap and let the dough rise until it has doubled in size, about 1 hour in a warm room.

3. Divide the dough into at least 24 pieces. They don't all need to be the same size and shape.

4. Spray an 8-inch square or round baking pan with baking spray.

5. Put the seeds in a small shallow bowl or on a plate. Roll the pieces of dough in the seeds, then pile them into the baking pan. You don't need to make an even layer, and you don't need to fit them into the edges of the pan—this is supposed to be a bumpy-lumpy interesting-looking bread.

6. Cover the pan with plastic wrap or place it in a large plastic bag and tie the open end closed. Refrigerate overnight or up to 24 hours.

ON BAKING DAY

1. Take the pan out of the refrigerator and heat the oven to 350°F.

2. Remove the plastic from the pan and bake the bread until it is nicely browned on the outside and the internal temperature of the loaf registers 195°F on an instant-read thermometer, about 45 minutes. Transfer the bread from the pan to a cooling rack and let cool for about 30 minutes before serving to pull apart; cool completely if slicing.

1 1/2 cups room temperature water

2 1/4 teaspoons active dry yeast

1 tablespoon sugar

4 cups (1 pound 2 ounces) bread flour

1 1/2 teaspoons kosher salt

2 tablespoons unsalted butter

1/4 teaspoon garlic powder (not garlic salt)

1/4 teaspoon powdered rosemary

1/2 teaspoon dry thyme

Nonstick baking spray

3 tablespoons white, brown, or toasted sesame seeds, poppy seeds, or a mixture of any of these

TIP

For the seeds, you can use any that you like or that you have on hand. You could also add finely chopped pine nuts or a good pinch of a very coarse salt to the mix.

MAPLE, BACON, *and* ONION LOAF

Maple, bacon, and onion make a lovely combination, with the maple adding sweetness, bacon adding its savory saltiness, and the toasted onion flakes adding their own distinct flavor.

For maximum flavor, look for grade B maple syrup, which is deeper and more intense than the more common grade A syrup. If you can't find it, grade A will be fine. Don't use pancake syrup. Most of them contain very little, if any, maple syrup.

Toasted onion flakes can be found at most supermarkets as well as specialty spice shops. It's the familiar topping that you often find on bagels, and it's a nice topping on burger buns and other breads too.

MAKES ONE 9 X 5-INCH LOAF

Nonstick baking spray

1 cup room temperature water

2 tablespoons grade B maple syrup

2$\frac{1}{4}$ teaspoons active dry yeast

3 cups (13$\frac{1}{2}$ ounces) bread flour, plus more as needed

2 tablespoons unsalted butter

$\frac{1}{2}$ teaspoon kosher salt

$\frac{1}{4}$ pound bacon, cooked until very crisp, drained, and crumbled

1 tablespoon toasted onion flakes

ON PREP DAY

1. Spray a 9 x 5-inch loaf pan with baking spray.

2. Combine all the ingredients in a stand mixer and knead with the dough hook until smooth. You can also mix the ingredients in a large bowl, then knead by hand.

3. Cover the bowl and set aside to rise until the dough has doubled in size, about 1 hour in a warm room.

4. Turn the dough out onto a lightly floured surface and pat it into a rough 8-inch square. Fold the top half to about the middle of the dough and press the edge down to secure it. Fold the top over again, this time to within about an inch or so of the bottom. Press the edge to seal. Now pull the bottom of the dough up to meet the dough roll you've created and seal the seam. Pinch the ends closed and place the dough, seam side down, in the prepared loaf pan.

5. Cover the pan with plastic wrap or place the whole pan in a large plastic bag and tie the open end shut. Refrigerate the bread overnight or up to 24 hours before baking.

ON BAKING DAY

1. Take the pan out of the refrigerator and heat the oven to 350°F.

2. Remove the plastic and bake the bread until it is nicely browned and the internal temperature reaches 195°F on an instant-read thermometer, about 1 hour. Turn out the bread from the pan and cool completely on a rack before slicing.

VARIATION

For something different, eliminate the toasted onion flakes and add $\frac{1}{2}$ cup of chopped walnuts.

TIP

Instead of crumbling bacon after cooking, cut it into small dice before cooking. Freeze the bacon for about 15 minutes to make cutting easier. Use a slotted spoon to remove the bacon pieces as they're done cooking and drain on a paper towel–lined plate.

SESAME-SEEDED SEMOLINA BREAD

Semolina flour is typically used for pasta making, but it's one of my favorite things to add to bread dough because it gives the bread a richer, more buttery flavor. The resulting bread also has a nice yellow tinge.

If you prefer, you can bake this bread in a 9 x 5-inch loaf pan instead of in a Dutch oven. On baking day, heat the oven to 350°F and bake the loaf until the interior reaches 195°F on an instant-read thermometer, about 50 minutes.

MAKES ONE 8- TO 10-INCH ROUND LOAF

ON PREP DAY

1. Spray the bottom and sides of a 3-quart or 5½-quart Dutch oven with baking spray, then sprinkle with cornmeal. The bread will spread to fill the width of the pan, so a bread baked in a larger pot will be shorter and wider than one baked in a smaller pot.

2. Combine all the ingredients (except the egg wash and sesame seeds) in a stand mixer and knead with the dough hook until smooth. You can also mix the ingredients in a large bowl, then knead by hand.

3. Cover the bowl and set aside to rise until the dough has doubled in size, about 1 hour in a warm room.

4. Flour your work surface lightly and turn out the dough. Knead briefly, then form the dough into a round ball. Place the ball, seam side down, in the Dutch oven. Cover the pot and refrigerate overnight or up to 24 hours.

ON BAKING DAY

1. Take the pot out of the refrigerator. Brush the top of the dough with the egg wash, then sprinkle with sesame seeds. Put the top of the Dutch oven back on the pot.

2. Place the Dutch oven in a cold oven and turn the heat to 400°F. Bake until the crust is browned and the internal temperature of the loaf reaches 195°F, about 50 minutes. Remove the pan from the oven and transfer the loaf to a rack to cool completely before slicing.

Nonstick baking spray

Cornmeal, for the pan

1 cup room temperature water

1 large egg

2¼ teaspoons active dry yeast

1 tablespoon sugar

2½ cups (11¼ ounces) bread flour, plus more as needed

1 cup (6 ounces) semolina flour

2 tablespoons unsalted butter

1½ teaspoons kosher salt

Egg wash (1 egg beaten with 1 tablespoon water)

2 tablespoons sesame seeds

TIP

If you only need a little bit of egg wash, such as for just one loaf, freeze the rest in a small container until you need it again.

STUFFING BREAD
with DRIED CRANBERRIES

Stuffing bread is not necessarily something you'd use to make stuffing. It is, however, the perfect bread for a turkey sandwich, even if the turkey is from the deli.

This bread has the flavors of fall, with sage from the poultry seasoning and herbs. The dried cranberries are optional, but add nice sweet-tangy nuggets to the bread. And the great thing about dried cranberries—often sold as Craisins®—is that you can find them year-round. If cranberries aren't your thing, this bread is also terrific with dried cherries or apricots.

MAKES ONE 9 X 5-INCH LOAF

1 cup room temperature water
1 teaspoon active dry yeast
2 1/2 cups (11 1/4 ounces) bread flour, plus more as needed
2 tablespoons sugar
2 teaspoons poultry seasoning
1 tablespoon dried parsley
1 teaspoon dried chives
1 teaspoon kosher salt
2 tablespoons unsalted butter
1/4 cup dried cranberries
Nonstick baking spray

ON PREP DAY

1. Combine all of the ingredients and knead by hand (mix first in a large bowl, then turn out and knead) or in a stand mixer fitted with the dough hook, until the dough is elastic.

2. Cover the bowl with plastic wrap, or place it in a large plastic bag and seal the ends. Refrigerate overnight or up to 24 hours.

ON BAKING DAY

1. Spray a 9 x 5-inch loaf pan with baking spray.

2. Turn the dough out onto a lightly floured surface and pat it into a rough 8-inch square. Fold the top half to about the middle of the dough and press the edge down to secure it. Fold the top over again, this time to within about an inch or so of the bottom. Press the edge to seal. Now pull the bottom of the dough up to meet the dough roll you've created and seal the seam. Pinch the ends closed and place the dough, seam side down, in the prepared pan.

3. Cover the pan with plastic wrap and set aside to rise. The dough is ready when it has risen about an inch over the top of the pan, about 1 hour in a warm room.

4. About 30 minutes before the loaf is fully risen, heat the oven to 350°F.

5. When the dough has risen, remove the plastic. Bake until the bread is richly browned and the internal temperature of the loaf reaches 195°F on an instant-read thermometer, about 55 minutes. Remove the bread from the pan and cool completely on a rack before slicing.

THREE CHEESE BREAD
with KALAMATA OLIVES

Olives and cheese are a great pair for snacking, and they work just as well together in this bread. It's great on its own in a breadbasket, and it makes a wonderful sandwich bread.

I like to use this bread for croutons, whether on salads or just for snacking, or for crostini. Since the cheese can melt out of the bread while you're oven-toasting it, use a silicone baking mat on the baking sheet. The cheese will still melt, but it won't stick to the pan and burn.

Store this bread in the refrigerator rather than at room temperature.

MAKES ONE 9 X 5-INCH LOAF

ON PREP DAY

1. Combine the water, yeast, sugar, flour, salt, and cream cheese in a stand mixer and knead with the dough hook until smooth. You can also mix the ingredients in a large bowl, then knead by hand.

2. When the dough is smooth, flour your work surface and turn out the dough. Add the Cheddar, Swiss, and olives, and knead them in. At first, the olives will make the dough feel wet and slick, but if you continue kneading, the dough will incorporate the ingredients.

3. Return the dough to the bowl. Cover the bowl and set aside to rise until the dough has doubled in size, about 1 hour in a warm room.

4. Spray a 9 x 5-inch loaf pan with baking spray.

5. Turn the dough out onto a lightly floured surface and pat it into a rough 8-inch square. Fold the top half to about the middle of the dough and press the edge down to secure it. Fold the top over again, this time to within about an inch or so of the bottom. Press the edge to seal. Now pull the bottom of the dough up to meet the dough roll you've created and seal the seam. Pinch the ends closed. If there are cubes of cheese poking all the way through the dough, push them in and pinch the hole closed. Place the dough, seam side down, in the prepared loaf pan.

6. Cover the pan with plastic wrap or place the whole pan in a large plastic bag and tie the open end shut. Refrigerate the bread overnight or up to 24 hours before baking.

ON BAKING DAY

1. Remove the pan from the refrigerator and heat the oven to 325°F.

2. Remove the plastic and bake the bread until it is nicely browned and the internal temperature reaches 195°F on an instant-read thermometer, about 50 minutes. Transfer the bread to a rack and cool completely before slicing.

1 cup room temperature water

2$\frac{1}{4}$ teaspoons active dry yeast

1 tablespoon sugar

3 cups (13$\frac{1}{2}$ ounces) bread flour, plus more as needed

1 teaspoon kosher salt

2 ounces cream cheese, at room temperature

4 ounces Cheddar cheese, cut into $\frac{1}{4}$-inch cubes

4 ounces Swiss cheese, cut into $\frac{1}{4}$-inch cubes

$\frac{1}{2}$ cup roughly chopped Kalamata olives, well drained

Nonstick baking spray

TIP

While this recipe calls for Kalamata olives, you can use any pitted olives you like—or a mix. Make sure the olives are well-drained, or you'll be adding extra liquid to the dough.

YEASTED JALAPEÑO *and* ROASTED RED PEPPER CORNBREAD

This cornbread will surprise you. While it has the same ratio of cornmeal to flour as many traditional cornbread recipes, the technique gives it the texture of a traditional yeasted bread. Roasted red peppers give up some of their color to the dough, so this bread is pretty and delicious.

If you don't like heat, substitute a bit of green bell pepper for all or some of the jalapeño, so you'll have the same pretty flecks of green without the spice.

Since the bread is made in mini loaf pans, you can cut thick or thin slices to slather with butter or make mini sandwiches or spicy crostini. Try a slice spread with cream cheese and topped with diced tomato or a sprinkle of chopped chives.

MAKES FOUR 5 X 3-INCH MINI LOAVES

ON PREP DAY

1. Combine all the ingredients in a stand mixer and knead with the dough hook until smooth. You can also mix the ingredients in a large bowl, then knead by hand. The red peppers add moisture to the dough, so if it is wet and sticky and won't form a cohesive ball, add a bit more flour (a tablespoon at a time) just until the dough comes together. If you are using a stand mixer, the dough should form a ball around the dough hook and clean the sides of the bowl. Don't worry if the dough seems too soft—the cornmeal in the dough will hydrate overnight, making the dough denser.

2. Cover the bowl with plastic wrap and set aside to rise until the dough has doubled in size, about 1 hour in a warm room.

3. Meanwhile, spray four 5 x 3-inch loaf pans with baking spray. You can also sprinkle them with cornmeal, for more corn flavor.

4. When the dough has risen, flour your work surface and turn out the dough. Divide it into four equal pieces. Form each piece into a log about 5 inches long, and place one log in each pan. Cover the pans with plastic wrap and refrigerate overnight or up to 24 hours.

ON BAKING DAY

1. Take the pans out of the refrigerator and heat the oven to 350°F.

2. Remove the plastic and bake the loaves until they are browned and the internal temperature reaches 195°F on an instant-read thermometer, about 30 minutes. Transfer the bread from the pans to a rack and let them cool completely before slicing.

1 cup room temperature water

2 1/4 teaspoons active dry yeast

1/4 cup sugar

1 egg

1/4 cup heavy cream

2 cups (9 ounces) bread flour, plus more as needed

2 cups (11 1/2 ounces) cornmeal, plus more for the pans (optional)

1 1/2 teaspoons kosher salt

1 cup diced roasted red peppers, well drained (about 1 large red pepper)

1 jalapeño, cored, seeded, and finely chopped

2 tablespoons butter

Nonstick baking spray

TIP

Cheese is a great addition to this bread; try it with 4 ounces of sharp Cheddar, cut into small cubes or coarsely shredded. Add it with the other ingredients; when forming the logs, poke down any pieces that stick up (if you use cubed cheese).

TOMATO *and* BLACK OLIVE BREAD

This bread adds zest to any sandwich. Try it as a grilled cheese with Cheddar and Mozzarella. Or with a BLT or just toast it and top with good feta and a drizzle of olive oil for a snack.

MAKES TWO 12-INCH ROUND LOAVES

1 cup room temperature water

1 teaspoon instant yeast

2 tablespoons sugar

5 to 5½ cups (1 pound 6½ ounces to 1 pound 8¾ ounces) bread flour, plus more as needed

1 cup tomato juice

1½ teaspoons kosher salt

One 6-ounce can pitted sliced black olives, drained well

3 tablespoons olive oil, divided

Cornmeal, for the pan

ON PREP DAY

1. Combine the water, yeast, sugar, 5 cups of flour, the tomato juice, and salt and knead by hand (mix first in a large bowl, then turn out and knead) or in a stand mixer fitted with the dough hook, until the dough is elastic.

2. Add the olives and 2 tablespoons of the olive oil and continue kneading until the olives are distributed throughout the dough. If the olives were very wet and the dough becomes very loose after adding them, add more flour, 1 tablespoon at a time. The dough should be soft, but not sticky. The dough will firm up a bit during refrigeration.

3. Drizzle the remaining 1 tablespoon of olive oil into a gallon-size zip-top plastic bag; place the dough in the bag and massage the bag a bit to coat the dough with the oil. Zip the bag closed and refrigerate overnight or up to 24 hours.

ON BAKING DAY

1. Remove the bag from the refrigerator, and sprinkle a baking sheet with cornmeal.

2. Dust your work surface lightly with flour and divide the dough in half. Form each half into a large ball. Hold one of the balls of dough with both hands, with the bottom of the dough resting on the counter. Turn the dough—clockwise or counter-clockwise, your choice—as though the dough is a large lightbulb and you're screwing it into the countertop. You'll feel the "skin" on the outside of the dough ball begin to tighten as you do this. When the outside of the dough ball feels firm, put it on the baking sheet. Repeat the process with the other dough ball and place it on the baking sheet, leaving room between them to rise. You can also opt to bake the loaves on two separate sheets to make sure they absolutely don't touch during baking.

3. Cover the loaves with plastic wrap and set the pan aside until the dough has doubled in size and when you poke the side with a fingertip, the indentation remains or fills in slowly, about 45 minutes in a warm room, depending on how cool the loaves were when you finished working with them.

4. About 30 minutes before the dough has finished rising, heat the oven to 350°F.

5. When the dough has risen, remove the plastic and bake the loaves until they are nicely browned and the internal temperature reaches 195°F on an instant-read thermometer, about 35 minutes. Let the loaves cool completely on a rack before slicing.

WHITE WHEAT LOAF

This is a great sandwich bread—it has all the goodness of whole wheat, it's soft but not mushy, and it's hearty enough for whatever you put on it.

This also makes terrific French toast because it stands up to soaking in the egg mixture without falling apart, and it's mild enough that it won't overpower the eggy flavor of the French toast.

MAKES ONE 9 X 5-INCH LOAF

ON PREP DAY

1. Combine all the ingredients in a stand mixer and knead with the dough hook until smooth. You can also mix the ingredients in a large bowl, then knead by hand.

2. Cover the bowl with plastic wrap and set aside to rise until the dough has doubled in size, about 1 hour in a warm room.

3. Meanwhile, spray a 9 x 5-inch loaf pan with baking spray.

4. Turn the dough out onto a lightly floured surface and pat it into a rough 8-inch square. Fold the top half to about the middle of the dough and press the edge down to secure it. Fold the top over again, this time to within about an inch or so of the bottom. Press the edge to seal. Now pull the bottom of the dough up to meet the dough roll you've created and seal the seam. Pinch the ends closed and place the dough, seam side down, in the prepared loaf pan.

5. Cover the pan with plastic wrap or place the whole pan in a large plastic bag and tie the open end shut. Refrigerate the bread overnight or up to 24 hours before baking.

ON BAKING DAY

1. Take the dough out of the refrigerator and heat the oven to 350°F.

2. Remove the plastic and bake the bread until it is nicely browned and the internal temperature reaches 205°F on an instant-read thermometer, about 55 minutes. Remove the bread from the pan and let it cool completely on a rack before slicing.

1 cup lukewarm water
$\frac{1}{4}$ cup nonfat dry milk
1 tablespoon sugar
$2\frac{1}{4}$ teaspoons active dry yeast
1 cup ($4\frac{1}{2}$ ounces) wheat flour
2 cups (9 ounces) bread flour, plus more as needed
$1\frac{1}{2}$ teaspoons kosher salt
2 tablespoons unsalted butter
Nonstick baking spray

TIP

This is a somewhat dense dough, so it can take a little extra time to double in size. If it needs an extra 10 minutes, give it the time; otherwise you won't get as much rise during refrigeration. If the loaf hasn't risen just a little over the top of the pan, you can give it a little more rising time just before baking.

PUMPKIN LOAF

Fresh pumpkins are available mainly in fall, but luckily for us, canned pumpkin is available year-round. It adds savory flavor and a lot of moistness to this slightly sweet loaf.

This is a great snacking bread but also makes a hearty yet quick breakfast when toasted and smeared with peanut butter, cream cheese, or a simple dab of butter.

MAKES ONE 8 X 4$\frac{1}{2}$-INCH LOAF

ON PREP DAY 1

Place all the ingredients in a gallon-size zip-top plastic bag and squeeze, squish, and massage the bag (with the top loosely closed) until they are combined. Close the bag and refrigerate the dough for 8 to 24 hours.

ON PREP DAY 2

1. Remove the dough from the refrigerator and let it rest on your kitchen counter until it has come to room temperature, at least 2 hours and up to 4 hours.

2. Flour your work surface and turn out the dough. Knead the dough until it is smooth and somewhat elastic, adding flour only as needed to keep it from sticking to your hands and the work surface. Because of the pumpkin, the dough won't be completely elastic.

3. Spray an 8 x 4$\frac{1}{2}$-inch loaf pan with baking spray and sprinkle cornmeal in the bottom of the pan.

4. Shape the dough into a log about 8 inches long and place it in the prepared pan. Cover the pan with plastic wrap or place it in a plastic bag and tie the end closed. Refrigerate overnight.

ON BAKING DAY

1. Take the pan out of the refrigerator and heat the oven to 350°F.

2. Remove the plastic from the pan and bake the bread until it is nicely browned and the internal temperature reaches 190°F on an instant-read thermometer, about 45 minutes. Turn out the bread onto a rack and let it cool before slicing.

2 cups (9 ounces) bread flour, plus more as needed
¼ cup honey
1 teaspoon active dry yeast
1 cup canned pumpkin (not pumpkin pie filling)
1 teaspoon kosher salt
1 tablespoon olive oil
Nonstick baking spray
Cornmeal, for the pan

TIP

Use a nut-based oil, like walnut or hazelnut, in place of the olive oil for extra flavor.

BLUEBERRY *and* CREAM CHEESE BUNS *with* LEMON ZEST

These buns are reminiscent of blueberry cheesecake, but in a sweet breakfast bread. When you look at a slice of one of the buns, it might look like the cream cheese has disappeared into the bread, but the flavor remains.

MAKES 12 BUNS

ON PREP DAY

1. Combine all of the dough ingredients and knead by hand (mix first in a large bowl, then turn out and knead) or in a stand mixer fitted with the dough hook, until the dough is elastic.

2. Cover the bowl with plastic wrap and let the dough rise until it has doubled in size, about 1 hour in a warm room.

3. Meanwhile, make the filling: Take the cream cheese out of the refrigerator and let it come to room temperature. When the cheese has softened, place it in a small bowl with the sugar, lemon zest, and 1 tablespoon milk. Mix well. You need a spreadable consistency, but it shouldn't be runny. Add more milk, if necessary.

4. Spray a 9 x 13 x 2-inch baking pan with baking spray.

5. When the dough has risen, flour your work surface and turn out the dough. Pat it into a rough square shape, then use a rolling pin to roll it to about 12 x 16 inches. Spread the cream cheese mixture on the dough in as even a layer as possible. It's easiest to dollop the mixture on, then spread it in that area rather than trying to spread it all from one large blob. An offset spatula works great for spreading. Leave about an inch of the dough uncovered on one of the long ends.

6. Sprinkle the blueberries evenly on top of the cream cheese.

7. Roll the dough, jellyroll style, beginning at the long end opposite the dough you left uncovered. Leave the roll a little bit loose as you go.

8. Cut the roll into 12 even pieces (each about 1 inch thick) and arrange them cut side up in the prepared baking pan.

9. Cover the pan with plastic wrap or place the whole pan in a large plastic bag and tie the open end closed. Refrigerate overnight or up to 24 hours.

ON BAKING DAY

1. Take the pan out of the refrigerator and heat the oven to 350°F.

2. Remove the plastic from the pan and bake the buns until they are golden-brown, about 40 minutes. If you're not sure the bread is fully baked, insert an instant-read thermometer into the bun dough—not filling; it should read 190°F.

3. Let the buns cool in the pan for 10 minutes, then transfer them to a rack to cool.

FOR THE DOUGH

1 egg, beaten, plus water to equal 1$\frac{1}{2}$ cups total

3$\frac{1}{2}$ cups (15$\frac{3}{4}$ ounces) bread flour, plus more as needed

$\frac{1}{4}$ cup brown sugar

2$\frac{1}{4}$ teaspoons active dry yeast

$\frac{1}{2}$ cup instant mashed potato flakes

$\frac{1}{4}$ cup nonfat dry milk

1 tablespoon pure vanilla extract

1$\frac{1}{2}$ teaspoons kosher salt

4 tablespoons unsalted butter

FOR THE FILLING

8 ounces cream cheese

2 tablespoons sugar

Zest of $\frac{1}{2}$ lemon

1 to 2 tablespoons milk

$\frac{1}{4}$ cup dried blueberries

Nonstick baking spray

VARIATION

If you like things sweet, add a drizzle of confectioners' sugar icing to the top of the buns after they've cooled. You can also switch out the blueberries for dried cherries.

TIP

Because of the cheese, these buns should be refrigerated for storage.

CINNAMON SWIRL BREAD

This is a basic, no-frills cinnamon bread that's great for breakfast or brunch. A day or two later, it's also perfect for French toast. Personally, my favorite way to eat it is toasted with just a small smear of butter.

The graham crackers are optional, but they add a nice texture to the filling and make it a little more substantial without being overly sweet.

MAKES TWO 8 X 4-INCH LOAVES

ON PREP DAY

1. Combine all of the dough ingredients and knead by hand (mix first in a large bowl, then turn out and knead) or in a stand mixer fitted with the dough hook, until the dough is elastic.

2. Cover the bowl with plastic wrap and let the dough rise until it has doubled in size, about 1 hour in a warm room.

3. Meanwhile, combine the filling ingredients in a small bowl. Spray two 8 x 4-inch loaf pans with baking spray

4. Divide the dough in half. Working with one half at a time, on a floured surface, pat the dough into a rough square, then use a rolling pin to roll the dough to a rectangle about 8 x 16 inches.

5. Sprinkle half the cinnamon sugar filling onto the dough rectangle, leaving about an inch uncovered on one of the short sides. Use the rolling pin to lightly press the mixture into the dough. Starting at the short side opposite the uncovered end, roll the dough, jellyroll style. When you reach the opposite side, pinch the dough to seal the seam, then pinch the ends of the roll closed as well. Place the finished dough in one of the prepared baking pans, seam side down. Cover the pan with plastic wrap or place the whole pan in a large plastic bag and tie the open end closed.

6. Prepare the second half of the dough in the same way.

7. Cover the pans with plastic wrap and place in the refrigerator overnight or up to 24 hours.

ON BAKING DAY

1. Remove the pans from the refrigerator and heat the oven to 350°F.

2. Remove the plastic from the pans and bake the loaves until they are nicely browned and the internal temperature reads 190°F, on an instant-read thermometer; make sure you test in the dough and not in the filling. Turn out the bread from the pans and let cool on a rack before slicing.

FOR THE DOUGH

4$\frac{1}{2}$ cups (20$\frac{1}{4}$ ounces) bread flour, plus more as needed

1$\frac{1}{2}$ cups lukewarm water

2 teaspoons active dry yeast

4 tablespoons sugar

8 tablespoons unsalted butter

1$\frac{1}{2}$ teaspoons kosher salt

1 egg

1 tablespoon pure vanilla extract

$\frac{1}{2}$ teaspoon almond extract

FOR THE FILLING

$\frac{1}{2}$ cup sugar

2 tablespoons ground cinnamon

2 graham crackers, crushed into crumbs (optional)

Nonstick baking spray

SWEET BUBBLE LOAF

There's something alluring about pulling apart a loaf of bread with your fingers, particularly when it tears into odd-shaped pieces. This bread is sweet enough to be a breakfast or brunch item, but not so sweet that it would replace dessert.

If you'd rather, slice this bread like a standard loaf. It won't fall apart and you'll see the veins of sugar in every slice. Because it's sweet, I don't recommend it for sandwiches, but it does make great French toast or bread pudding.

MAKES ONE 9 X 5-INCH LOAF

3 cups (13½ ounces) bread flour, plus more as needed

1 teaspoon instant yeast

½ cup cane sugar, divided

1 teaspoon kosher salt

4 tablespoons unsalted butter

1 tablespoon pure vanilla extract

¼ cup nonfat dry milk

Nonstick baking spray

Cornmeal, for the pan

ON PREP DAY

1. Mix all of the ingredients in a large bowl, using just ¼ cup of the sugar and reserving the other ¼ cup. There's no need to knead, just mix well. Cover the bowl with plastic wrap and let the mixture rest for 45 minutes.

2. Flour your work surface and turn out the dough. Knead it briefly—it should become elastic very quickly.

3. Divide the dough into 8 pieces. Divide each of those 8 pieces in half, thirds, or quarters, so that you have a variety of different-sized pieces. Roll each of those pieces into a ball.

4. Spray a 9 x 5-inch loaf pan with baking spray and sprinkle cornmeal on the bottom.

5. Place the remaining ¼ cup sugar in a shallow bowl. For the first layer of dough balls, dip each ball into the sugar and place the balls sugar side up in the pan. Continue rolling dough balls in the sugar to coat them completely before placing them in the pan. Scatter them haphazardly in the pan, but try to keep the overall height somewhat even. If you need more sugar to coat all the balls, add more. If there is sugar left over, you can sprinkle it on top of the loaf when you're finished.

6. Cover the pan with plastic wrap or place the whole pan in a large plastic bag and tie the open end closed. Refrigerate overnight or up to 24 hours.

ON BAKING DAY

1. Take the pan out of the refrigerator and heat the oven to 325°F.

2. Uncover the pan and bake the bread at 325°F until the top is very brown and the internal temperature reaches 190°F on an instant-read thermometer, about 50 minutes. Check partway through baking and if the top seems to be browning too quickly, cover the pan with some foil. Remove the bread from the oven, turn it out of the pan, and let it cool on a rack. You can slice this bread or tear off pieces.

ALMOND SWEET BREAD

This bread, because of the filling, reminds me a lot of sweet breads and pastries that my mom would buy from a local bakery when I was a kid. Sometimes she'd suspect that they substituted pecan for the almond. At the time, I didn't understand that nuts have different flavors. But Mom knew—she was particularly fond of almond filling, even though she normally wasn't a fan of sweets. This bread pays homage to those memories.

MAKES ONE 8-INCH ROUND LOAF

1 cup room temperature water

One 12½-ounce can almond cake and pastry filling, divided

2¼ teaspoons active dry yeast

3 cups (13½ ounces) bread flour, plus more as needed

1 teaspoon kosher salt

4 tablespoons unsalted butter

½ cup nonfat dry milk

ON PREP DAY

1. Combine the water, ½ cup (about half of the 12 ½-ounce can) of almond filling, the yeast, flour, salt, butter, and dry milk in a stand mixer. Knead with the bread hook until the dough is smooth and elastic. You can also mix the ingredients in a large bowl, then knead by hand.

2. Cover the bowl with plastic wrap and set aside to rise until the dough has doubled in size, about 1 hour in a warm room.

3. Flour your work surface and turn out the dough. Divide the dough in half, and form each piece into a ball. Place one ball on a piece of parchment paper cut to fit a baking sheet.

4. Using a rolling pin, roll the other ball into an 8-inch diameter circle. Spread the remaining almond filling on the dough circle, covering the surface evenly to within about ½ inch of the edges.

5. On a lightly floured surface, roll the second dough ball to the same size, 8 inches in diameter. Place this round on top of the first one and pinch the edges to seal them. Place the round on a parchment-lined baking sheet, cover the pan with plastic wrap, and refrigerate the dough overnight or up to 24 hours.

ON BAKING DAY

1. Remove the pan from the refrigerator and heat the oven to 350°F.

2. Remove the plastic and bake the bread until it's nicely browned and the internal temperature reaches 190°F on an instant-read thermometer, about 40 minutes. Transfer the bread, on the parchment, to a rack to cool completely before slicing into wedges to serve.

TIP

There are a number of different prepared almond products available. Almond paste is probably the most common, but almond cake and pastry filling is readily available at most grocery stores. Look for it near the pie fillings.

SWEET POTATO MONKEY BREAD

Sweet potatoes are a wonderful addition to bread dough—they add sweetness, color, and flavor. These days, sweet potatoes aren't just orange. You can find them in a brighter orange, an almost-red, or a paler yellow, and even a deep purple color. Any of them are good for this recipe, depending on what color you want your bread to be.

This is a perfect recipe for leftover baked or roasted sweet potatoes, or you can bake a potato specifically for use in the bread. Just wrap the potato in aluminum foil and bake at 350°F until the potato is very soft, an hour or more depending on its size. Or poke holes in the potato and microwave it until it's soft.

If you're using leftover mashed sweet potatoes that you've added butter or spices to, keep in mind that those flavorings will also flavor the bread. Unless you've added something very strange, the taste should be just fine, though.

Don't use canned yams in this recipe—they're too watery, even after they're well drained.

MAKES ONE 8-INCH ROUND OR SQUARE LOAF

FOR THE DOUGH

- 1/2 cup cooked sweet potato flesh
- 1 egg
- 1/2 cup sugar
- 2 1/4 teaspoons active dry yeast
- 1/2 cup room temperature water
- 2 1/2 cups (11 1/4 ounces) bread flour
- 4 tablespoons unsalted butter
- 1 teaspoon kosher salt

Nonstick baking spray

FOR THE COATING

- 3 tablespoon hazelnut meal (or almond meal)
- 3 tablespoons sugar
- 3 tablespoons graham cracker crumbs
- 1 teaspoon ground cinnamon

ON PREP DAY

1. Combine all of the dough ingredients and knead by hand (mix first in a large bowl, then turn out and knead) or in a stand mixer fitted with the dough hook, until the dough is elastic.

2. Cover the bowl with plastic wrap and let the dough rise until it has doubled in size, about 1 hour in a warm room.

3. Divide the dough into at least 24 pieces. They don't all need to be the same size, and in fact I encourage you to make them random. Cut more than 24 pieces if you like.

4. Spray an 8-inch round or square baking pan with baking spray.

5. Combine the coating ingredients in a small shallow bowl or plate and roll each piece of dough in the coating, then pile them into the prepared baking pan. You don't need to make an even layer, and you don't need them to go all the way to the edges of the pan—this is supposed to be a bumpy-lumpy interesting-looking bread.

6. Cover the pan with plastic wrap or place it in a large plastic bag and tie the open end closed. Place the pan in the refrigerator overnight or up to 24 hours.

ON BAKING DAY

1. Remove the pan from the refrigerator and heat the oven to 325°F.

2. Remove the plastic and bake the bread until it is nicely browned and the internal temperature registers 190°F on an instant-read thermometer, about 45 minutes. Let the bread cool in the pan for a few minutes, then transfer to a rack to cool for another 20 minutes or so before serving.

CANDIED-GINGER BREAD

When you think of ginger in bread, the first thing that comes to mind is probably the gingerbread-man flavored confections, but this bread is nothing like those cookies. There are no cloves, cinnamon, or molasses. Instead, the ginger is complemented by the flavors of peanut and almond.

While this bread is sweet enough to be a breakfast bread, its flavors go very well with spicy foods, particularly Thai-inspired dishes where peanuts and ginger often go hand in hand.

The size of the ginger and peanuts is up to you, but I suggest you shoot for bits about the size of lentils for best distribution throughout the bread.

MAKES ONE 9 X 5-INCH LOAF

ON PREP DAY

1. Combine all the ingredients in a stand mixer and knead with the dough hook until smooth. You can also mix the ingredients in a large bowl, then knead by hand.

2. Cover the bowl with plastic wrap and set aside to rise until the dough has doubled in size, about 1 hour in a warm room. This dough can rise a little slowly, so it could take up to 90 minutes for the first rise.

3. Meanwhile, spray a 9 x 5-inch loaf pan with baking spray.

4. Turn the dough out onto a lightly floured surface and pat it into a rough 8-inch square. Fold the top half to about the middle of the dough and press the edge down to secure it. Fold the top over again, this time to within about an inch or so of the bottom. Press the edge to seal. Now pull the bottom of the dough up to meet the dough roll you've created and seal the seam. Pinch the ends closed and place the dough, seam side down, in the prepared loaf pan.

5. Cover the pan with plastic wrap or place the whole pan in a large plastic bag and tie the open end shut. Refrigerate the bread overnight or up to 24 hours before baking.

ON BAKING DAY

1. Take the pan out of the refrigerator and heat the oven to 325°F.

2. Remove the plastic and bake the loaf until it is nicely browned and the internal temperature reaches 190°F on an instant-read thermometer, about 65 minutes. Remove the bread from the pan and cool completely on a rack before slicing.

1 cup room temperature water
$1/4$ cup honey
$2 1/4$ teaspoons active dry yeast
3 cups ($13 1/2$ ounces) bread flour, plus more as needed
$1 1/2$ teaspoons kosher salt
2 tablespoons unsalted butter
$1/2$ cup chopped candied ginger
1 teaspoon almond extract
$1/4$ cup chopped peanuts
Nonstick baking spray

TIP

Candied ginger can be a little difficult to chop, because it tends to stick to the knife. To make it a little easier, you can sprinkle some of the flour from the recipe onto the cutting board and on the ginger pieces. Or spray the knife with nonstick spray, wipe it with a paper towel, and then chop.

MAPLE SUGAR *and* CANDIED WALNUT SWIRL BREAD

This loaf features candied walnuts. Take my advice and make a double batch of walnuts just for snacking—they're pretty darned good.

Since maple sugar can be a little pricey I used regular granulated sugar and maple syrup for the candied walnuts, with just a little bit of maple sugar on top.

For a different look, pearl sugar would also make a nice topping.

MAKES ONE 9 X 5-INCH LOAF

ON PREP DAY

1. Make the candied walnuts: Combine the granulated sugar, maple syrup, and walnuts in a small sauté pan. Heat on medium, stirring as needed, until all the sugar is melted and it begins to bubble. Take the pan off the heat and transfer the candied walnuts to a plate. Let cool, then break into pieces.

2. Make the dough: Combine the water, yeast, granulated sugar, butter, flour, salt, and potato flakes in a stand mixer fitted with the dough hook and knead until smooth. You can also mix the ingredients in a medium bowl, then knead by hand.

3. Flour your work surface lightly, then turn out the dough. Knead the candied walnuts (and any extra sugar clinging to the pan) in by hand, kneading just enough to incorporate and distribute the walnuts and sugar. You don't want the sugar to completely mix into the dough or you won't get the pretty sugary streaks.

4. Return the dough to the bowl, cover with plastic wrap, and let the dough rise until it has doubled in size, about 1 hour in a warm room.

5. Spray a 9 x 5-inch loaf pan with nonstick baking spray.

6. Turn the dough out onto a lightly floured surface and pat it into a rough 8-inch square. Fold the top half to about the middle of the dough and press the edge down to secure it. Fold the top over again, this time to within about an inch or so of the bottom. Press the edge to seal. Now pull the bottom of the dough up to meet the dough roll you've created and seal the seam. Pinch the ends closed and place the dough, seam side down, in the prepared loaf pan.

7. Cover the pan with plastic wrap or place the whole pan in a large plastic bag and tie the open end shut. Refrigerate overnight or up to 24 hours before baking.

ON BAKING DAY

1. Take the pan out of the refrigerator and heat the oven to 325°F.

2. Remove the plastic, brush the top of the loaf with the egg wash, and sprinkle with the maple sugar. Bake the bread until it is nicely browned and the internal temperature reaches 190°F on an instant-read thermometer, about 1 hour. Remove the bread from the pan and let it cool completely on a rack before slicing.

FOR THE CANDIED WALNUTS

1/4 cup granulated sugar

2 tablespoons maple syrup

1/2 cup chopped walnuts

FOR THE DOUGH

1 1/4 cups room temperature water

2 1/4 teaspoons active dry yeast

1/4 cup granulated sugar

4 tablespoons unsalted butter

3 cups (13 1/2 ounces) bread flour, plus more as needed

1 1/2 teaspoons kosher salt

1/4 cup instant mashed potato flakes

Nonstick baking spray

Egg wash (1 egg beaten with 1 tablespoon water)

1 tablespoon maple sugar

TIP

If you're kneading by hand, it's best if you use softened butter. But if you're using a stand mixer, it has enough power to incorporate refrigerator-temperature butter into the dough, and the friction from kneading will make sure it's soft rather than in chunks. The kneading will take a little longer, but not very much.

PEANUT BUTTER BREAD
with RASPBERRY SWIRL

I love peanut butter bread. The peanut flavor is so appealing and when it's in the toaster, the house smells like I'm roasting peanuts. Of course, you don't have to use peanut butter in this recipe. Any nut butter, or non-nut butter like sunflower seed butter, will work perfectly well.

To make this bread even more special, a swirl of raspberry jam turns it into a peanut butter and jelly delight, all in one slice. Use a thick jam or fruit spread—the thicker the better. Jelly would make an unpleasant mess.

MAKES ONE 9 X 5-INCH LOAF

ON PREP DAY

1. Combine all of the dough ingredients except the jam and knead by hand (mix first in a large bowl, then turn out and knead) or in a stand mixer fitted with the dough hook, until the dough is elastic.

2. Cover the bowl with plastic wrap and let the dough rise for an hour in a warm room. If it hasn't doubled in size, that's perfectly fine, but you should see that it has risen and is puffier.

3. Spray a 9 x 5-inch loaf pan with baking spray and flour your work surface lightly (you might not need any at all, but a little doesn't hurt). Pat the dough to a rough square, then use a rolling pin to roll the dough to a rectangle about 10 x 15 inches.

4. Spread the jam on the dough, leaving about an inch uncovered on one of the short sides. Starting at the short side opposite the uncovered end, roll the dough, jellyroll style. When you reach the opposite side, pinch the dough to seal the seam, then pinch the ends of the roll closed as well. Place the finished dough in the prepared baking pan, seam side down. Flatten the dough slightly so it just touches the sides of the pan. Don't mash, just press lightly.

5. Cover the pan with plastic wrap or place the whole pan in a large plastic bag and tie the open end closed. Refrigerate overnight or up to 24 hours.

ON BAKING DAY

1. Take the pan out of the refrigerator and heat the oven to 350°F.

2. Remove the plastic from the pan and bake the loaf until it is nicely browned and the internal temperature registers 190°F on an instant-read thermometer inserted in the center making sure it's in the dough and not in the filling. Transfer the bread to a rack and let cool before slicing.

1 cup room temperature water
$2^{1}/_{4}$ teaspoons active dry yeast
$^{1}/_{4}$ cup sugar
$2^{1}/_{2}$ cups ($11^{1}/_{4}$ ounces) bread flour, plus more as needed
$^{1}/_{2}$ cup smooth peanut butter
1 teaspoon kosher salt
Nonstick baking spray
$1^{1}/_{2}$ cups raspberry jam

OATMEAL-CHERRY-WALNUT LOAF

This slightly sweet bread isn't dessert-sweet. Try it toasted with a smear of cream cheese or with ham, turkey, or tuna salad for a sandwich.

If you use this bread to make French toast (it's really good!), consider serving it with raspberry syrup or jam in place of the traditional maple syrup.

Walnuts tend to make breads darker, so don't be surprised at the color.

MAKES ONE 9 X 5-INCH LOAF

ON PREP DAY

1. Combine the water, yeast, honey, oats, bread flour, salt, and butter in a stand mixer and knead with the dough hook until smooth. You can also mix the ingredients in a large bowl, then knead by hand. Add the cherries and walnuts and knead just long enough to incorporate them into the dough, whether by hand or machine.

2. Cover the bowl with plastic wrap and set aside to rise until the dough has doubled in size, about 1 hour in a warm room.

3. Spray a 9 x 5-inch loaf pan with baking spray.

4. Turn the dough out onto a lightly floured surface and pat it into a rough 8-inch square. Fold the top half to about the middle of the dough and press the edge down to secure it. Fold the top over again, this time to within about an inch or so of the bottom. Press the edge to seal. Now pull the bottom of the dough up to meet the dough roll you've created and seal the seam. Pinch the ends closed and place the dough, seam side down, in the prepared loaf pan.

5. Cover the pan with plastic wrap or place the whole pan in a large plastic bag and tie the open end shut. Refrigerate overnight or up to 24 hours before baking.

ON BAKING DAY

1. Take the dough out of the refrigerator and heat the oven to 325°F.

2. Remove the plastic and bake the bread until it is nicely browned and the internal temperature reaches 195°F on an instant-read thermometer, about 55 minutes. Transfer the bread to a rack and let it cool completely before slicing.

1 cup water
2 1/4 teaspoons active dry yeast
1/4 cup honey
1 1/2 cups quick-cooking oats
2 cups (9 ounces) bread flour, plus more as needed
1 teaspoon kosher salt
4 tablespoons unsalted butter
1/2 cup dried cherries
1/2 cup roughly chopped walnuts
Nonstick baking spray

TIP

Try this recipe with other dried fruits like apricots or cranberries. Slivered almonds, pecans, or sunflower seeds could be used in place of the walnuts.

STRAWBERRY JAM SWIRL

This bread has a double dose of jam—some in the dough and some in the swirl. Because of the higher sugar content, this can be a slow-rising bread, so look for a warm place for it to rise the first time, or be prepared to wait. If your oven isn't in use, that's a good place to let dough rise. Just leave the light on, and it will create a warm environment without being too warm.

If you're using jam straight from the fridge, that chill will also lengthen the rise time, so compensate for that by using slightly warmer water.

Don't be tempted to add extra jam to the swirl, as that can cause unwanted gaps in the bread.

MAKES ONE 9 X 5-INCH LOAF

ON PREP DAY

1. Combine the water, sugar, egg, flour, salt, butter, and ¼ cup of jam in a stand mixer fitted with the dough hook. You can also mix in a large bowl, then knead by hand until the dough is smooth. Cover the bowl with plastic and set aside to rise until the dough has doubled in size, up to 2 hours at room temperature. For a faster rise, find a warm—but not hot—place to let the dough rise.

2. Spray a 9 x 5-inch loaf pan with baking spray.

3. Flour your work surface and turn out the dough. Form it into a rough square, then use a rolling pin to roll it to approximately 8 x 18 inches.

4. Spread the remaining jam evenly on the dough, leaving about 2 inches uncovered on one of the short ends of the dough.

5. Roll the dough, jellyroll style, starting at the short end opposite the uncovered end. When the roll reaches the far end, pinch to seal the seam, then pinch the ends of the roll closed, making sure there's no jam seeping through—leaking jam is likely to burn during baking. Place the roll, seam side down, in the prepared pan.

6. Cover the pan with plastic wrap or place the whole pan in a large plastic bag and tie the open end shut. Refrigerate overnight or up to 24 hours before baking. The dough should be fully risen after about 8 hours, but a longer rest is good for it.

ON BAKING DAY

1. Take the dough out of the refrigerator and heat the oven to 325°F.

2. Remove the plastic and bake the bread until it is nicely browned and the internal temperature reaches 190°F on an instant-read thermometer, about 65 minutes. Remove the bread from the pan and cool completely on a rack before slicing.

¾ cup room temperature water

¼ cup sugar

1 egg

3½ cups (15¾ ounces) bread flour, plus more as needed

1½ teaspoons kosher salt

4 tablespoons unsalted butter

½ cup strawberry jam, divided

Nonstick baking spray

TIP

Look for a thick, chunky jam rather than one that has a smooth, jelly-like texture. Thinner jams tend to cause the dough to separate at the swirl. The bread will still taste good, but it's not as pretty a presentation.

BUNS, ROLLS & BREADSTICKS

WHITE-WHOLE WHEAT HONEY VANILLA BUNS

Vanilla might seem like an odd ingredient in a bun that's not sweet, but it adds a subtle flavor that works to counteract the earthiness of the whole wheat. In the same way, using 50/50 flour adds the healthfulness of whole wheat with the more palatable texture and flavor of white. The 50/50 flour blends are available at the market, so home cooks no longer have to make their own. If you don't want to buy a blended flour, however, just use half all-purpose white and half whole wheat.

MAKES 9 BUNS

1 cup warm water
1 teaspoon instant yeast
2 tablespoons honey
3 cups (13½ ounces) 50/50 flour (half white flour and half whole wheat), plus more as needed
¼ cup nonfat dry milk
1 teaspoon kosher salt
1 teaspoon pure vanilla extract
1 tablespoon olive oil
Nonstick baking spray

ON PREP DAY

1. Combine all of the ingredients and by hand (mix first in a large bowl, then turn out and knead) or in a stand mixer fitted with the dough hook, until the dough is elastic. It will be a little "bumpy" from the small bits of whole wheat, but the dough itself should be smooth rather than shaggy.

2. Cover the bowl with plastic wrap and let the dough rise until it has doubled in size, about 1 hour in a warm room.

3. Flour your work surface and turn out the dough. Divide it into 9 equal pieces and form them into round balls.

4. Spray a 9 inch square baking pan with baking spray and arrange the dough balls in 3 rows of 3 in the pan. Cover the pan with plastic wrap or place the whole pan in a large plastic bag and tie the open end closed. Refrigerate overnight or up to 24 hours.

ON BAKING DAY

1. Take the pan out of the refrigerator and heat the oven to 350°F.

2. Remove the plastic and bake the buns until nicely browned and the internal temperature registers 205°F on an instant-read thermometer, about 35 minutes. Transfer to a wire rack until cool.

WHITE WHEAT POPPYSEED BUNS

These are the perfect buns to put in the bread basket for people who like whole grain breads as well as for those who prefer light, fluffy, all-white buns. White wheat flour is a whole grain product and it adds some color to the buns, but the flavor isn't as strong as the standard whole wheat flour that's made from red wheat. Meanwhile, poppy seeds add crunch and flavor as well as visual interest.

MAKES 12 BUNS

ON PREP DAY

1. Combine all of the ingredients except the egg wash and poppyseeds and knead by hand (mix first in a large bowl, then turn out and knead) or in a stand mixer fitted with the dough hook until the dough is elastic.

2. Cover the bowl with plastic wrap and let the dough rise until it has doubled in size, about 1 hour in a warm room.

3. Spray a 9 x 13-inch baking pan with nonstick spray.

4. Flour your work surface and turn out the dough. Divide the dough into 12 pieces and form them into rounds. Arrange the buns in the pan in 4 rows of 3 buns.

5. Cover the pan with plastic wrap or put the pan in a large plastic bag and tie the end closed. Refrigerate overnight.

ON BAKING DAY

1. Remove the pan from the refrigerator and heat the oven to 350°F.

2. Remove the plastic from the pan. Brush the buns with the egg wash and sprinkle with the poppyseeds, then bake the buns until they are a dark golden-brown and the internal temperature registers 205°F on an instant-read thermometer, about 35 minutes. Transfer the buns from the pan to a wire rack and let cool.

---

1 $\frac{1}{4}$ cups room temperature water

2 $\frac{1}{4}$ teaspoons active dry yeast

1 $\frac{1}{2}$ cups (6 $\frac{3}{4}$ ounces) white wheat flour

2 cups (9 ounces) bread flour, plus more as needed

1 tablespoon honey

1 teaspoon kosher salt

1 tablespoon olive oil

Nonstick baking spray

Egg wash (1 large egg beaten with 1 tablespoon water)

$\frac{1}{3}$ cup poppyseeds

GLUTEN-FREE DINNER ROLLS

These days, just about everyone knows someone who is eating gluten-free, so it's good to have a few recipes at your disposal.

Many gluten-free yeast bread recipes get one rise and then they go right into the oven. That's because there's no gluten that needs developing. However, there are still advantages to letting the dough rest overnight before baking. First, the resulting bread has a yeastier flavor, which is something I find appealing. And second, some gluten-free flours tend to have a gritty feel. The long rest softens those flours, which improves the bread texture.

There are many gluten-free flour mixes on the market these days. I used the King Arthur Flour gluten-free multipurpose flour since it was highly recommended by several gluten-free friends and is available at many grocery stores.

MAKES 12 ROLLS

ON PREP DAY

1. Spray a 12-cup muffin pan with cooking spray (not baking spray, which contains flour) or use butter or oil to grease the muffin cups.

2. Combine all the ingredients in a stand mixer fitted with the paddle attachment, or combine in a medium bowl and beat with an electric mixer. Mix for 5 minutes. You'll end up with something that is the consistency of mashed potatoes gone wrong.

3. Divide the dough evenly among the 12 muffin cups. You can smooth the tops if you want a more bun-like appearance, or leave the tops a little pointy and ragged for more interesting browning patterns.

4. Cover the pan with plastic wrap or place it in a large plastic bag and tie the open end closed. Let it rest at room temperature for 30 minutes, then refrigerate overnight or up to 24 hours.

ON BAKING DAY

1. Take the pan out of the refrigerator and heat the oven to 375°F.

2. Remove the plastic and bake the rolls until the tops are lightly browned and the internal temperature is 205°F on an instant read thermometer, about 35 minutes. If you want a little more browning, brush the tops of the rolls with melted butter about halfway through the cooking time.

3. Flip the buns out of the pan onto a wire rack and let cool completely.

Nonstick cooking spray

2 large eggs

1¼ cups room temperature water

2¼ teaspoons active dry yeast

3 cups (16½ ounces) gluten-free multipurpose flour

¼ cup cornstarch

2 teaspoons kosher salt

4 tablespoons unsalted butter, plus more for browning the tops (optional)

1 tablespoon xanthan gum

2 tablespoons sugar

TIP

Gluten-free breads can be a bit bland, so feel free to add herbs, spices, or flavorings to complement the rest of the meal. Just make sure that what you're adding is indeed safe for your friends who need to avoid gluten.

PUMPKIN DINNER ROLLS

Pumpkin isn't just for Thanksgiving! These rolls are a great addition to any fall or winter dinner table. The orange color makes them a little more interesting than a plain white dinner roll, and the subtle pumpkin flavor makes them a little more savory.

Even when pumpkins are in season, I prefer to buy canned pure pumpkin because it's a more consistent product. The water content of fresh pumpkin or other squash can vary a lot, which impacts the bread's hydration. If you do decide to cook your own pumpkin, look for pie pumpkins, which are small varieties with names like 'Small Sugar Pumpkin', 'New England Pie Pumpkin', 'Autumn Gold', and 'Baby Pam'.

Use leftover rolls to make the Maple Pecan Bread Pudding on p. 174.

MAKES 12 ROLLS

ON PREP DAY

1. Line a baking sheet with parchment paper or sprinkle with cornmeal.

2. Combine all the ingredients in a stand mixer and knead with the dough hook until smooth. You can also mix the ingredients in a large bowl, using a hand-held electric mixer, then knead by hand.

3. Cover the bowl with plastic wrap and set aside to rise until the dough has doubled in size, about 1 hour.

4. Flour your work surface and turn out the dough. Divide it into 12 equal pieces and roll each piece into a ball. Arrange the balls on the prepared baking pan and cover the pan with plastic wrap or place it in a large plastic bag and tie the open end closed. Refrigerate overnight or up to 24 hours.

ON BAKING DAY

1. Take the pan out of the refrigerator and heat the oven to 350°F.

2. Remove the plastic and bake the rolls until nicely browned and the internal temperature is 205°F on an instant-read thermometer, about 30 minutes. Transfer to a wire rack and let cool.

Cornmeal, for the pan (optional)

1 cup canned pure pumpkin

$1/2$ cup room temperature water

$2^1/4$ teaspoons active dry yeast

2 tablespoons honey

$3^1/2$ cups ($15^3/4$ ounces) bread flour, plus more as needed

$1/4$ cup nonfat dry milk

2 tablespoons unsalted butter

1 teaspoon kosher salt

TIP

If you want to add something extra to these rolls, try a teaspoon of thyme (fresh, finely minced, or dried) or $1/4$ cup of chopped walnuts. Both are delicious.

YEASTED AEBLESKIVERS

Aebleskivers are a Danish pastry, often served at the holidays. Traditional aebleskivers (or balls) are like pancakes in color and texture, but these definitely show their relationship to yeast breads. Aebleskivers aren't baked—they are cooked on the stovetop in an aebleskiver pan that is made from cast iron and has round wells. Since a pan only makes 7 aebleskivers at a time, you'll need to work in batches.

The slightly difficult part in making aebleskivers is figuring out exactly when to turn the buns over and how to do it smoothly. A sturdy wooden skewer is the best tool I've found for the turning.

MAKES 21 BUNS

1½ cups (6¾ ounces) unbleached all-purpose flour
1 tablespoon sugar
¼ teaspoon kosher salt
1 teaspoon instant yeast
½ cup milk
½ cup room temperature water
1 large egg
Vegetable oil, for the pan

ON PREP DAY

Combine all of the ingredients except the vegetable oil in a medium bowl and mix well, making sure everything is evenly mixed and there are no dry bits. Cover the bowl with plastic wrap and refrigerate overnight.

ON BAKING DAY

1. Remove the bowl from the refrigerator.

2. Heat your aebleskiver pan on medium heat until a drop of water sizzles when it hits the pan. Pour a small amount of vegetable oil in a small bowl and use a silicone brush to very lightly oil each well of the pan.

3. Use a small dish or spoon to fill each well of the aebleskiver pan with batter to about three-quarters full; the buns will rise as they cook. Let them cook for 2 to 3 minutes—you should see bubbles rising to the top, as you would with pancakes.

4. Test one aebleskiver to see if it is ready to turn: Insert a skewer into an aebleskiver and try to spin it in the well. If it doesn't release easily, continue cooking until it does (test again after another minute). Once the aebleskivers are willing to release from the wells, use the skewer to turn them over in the pan. Some of the batter might "spill" into the pan—that's fine.

5. Continue cooking the aebleskivers, turning them as needed, until they are evenly browned on the outside and cooked through on the inside—you'll have to break one open to check. You might need to lower the heat if the aebleskivers brown too quickly on the outside before they are thoroughly cooked inside.

6. When the first panful is cooked, remove the aebleskivers and let cool on a wire rack, brush the wells with oil as before, and continue cooking in batches until all the batter is used.

Yeasted Aebleskivers with Stone Fruit and Almond Jam. *(recipe on p. 192)*

BUTTER BUNS

These buns are loaded with butter, so you probably won't want to add any when you eat them. They're amazing as dinner rolls, but they're also terrific for breakfast, spread with jam, or used to sop up sunny-side-up eggs.

This recipe is difficult to knead by hand. The first mixture is very dense and would be hard to hand-knead, and it's next to impossible to incorporate the butter by hand. This recipe is a delicious excuse to buy that stand mixer you've always wanted.

MAKES 12

ON PREP DAY

1. Spray a 9 x 1-inch baking pan with nonstick baking spray.

2. Combine the water, sugar, yeast, flour, and salt in a stand mixer and knead with the dough hook until smooth. Add the butter, 1 tablespoon at a time, letting each tablespoon incorporate into the dough before adding the next.

3. Cover the bowl and set the dough aside to rise until it has doubled in size, about 1 hour.

4. Flour your work surface and turn out the dough. Divide it into 12 equal pieces and roll each piece into a ball.

5. Arrange the balls on the prepared baking pan and cover it with plastic wrap or place it in a large plastic bag and tie the open end closed. Refrigerate overnight or up to 24 hours.

ON BAKING DAY

1. Take the dough out of the refrigerator and heat the oven to 350°F.

2. Remove the plastic and bake the buns until nicely browned and the internal temperature is 190°F on an instant-read thermometer, about 25 minutes. Transfer to a wire rack to cool.

Nonstick baking spray
1 cup room temperature water
1 tablespoon sugar
2$\frac{1}{4}$ teaspoons active dry yeast
3 cups (13$\frac{1}{2}$ ounces) bread flour, plus more as needed
1 teaspoon kosher salt
1 stick (8 tablespoons) unsalted butter

TIP

If you have leftovers, use these buns to make Individual Stuffed French Toast (recipe on p. 175).

PAR-BAKED WHITE ROLLS

When I was a kid, we weren't big on family traditions, but one thing you could count on for Thanksgiving and Christmas was that Mom would buy par-baked buns and bake them right before dinner so they could be served warm. She'd take the turkey or roast out of the oven to rest, and the buns would go in. The meat would get carved, the sides would get plated, everything would get served, and everyone would dig in. And then sure as the sun rises every day, Mom would leap up and shriek, "THE BUNS!" And just like the year before, we'd be served buns with blackened bottoms.

These buns pay homage to those buns. You can bake them well ahead of time and brown them right before serving.

MAKES 12 ROLLS

1 large egg plus room temperature water to equal 1$^1/_2$ cups
2$^1/_4$ teaspoons instant yeast
3 tablespoons sugar
$^1/_2$ cup instant mashed potatoes
$^1/_2$ cup nonfat dry milk
3 cups (13$^1/_2$ ounces) bread flour, plus more as needed
1$^1/_2$ teaspoons kosher salt
2 tablespoons unsalted butter, at room temperature
Nonstick baking spray

ON PREP DAY 1

1. Combine all of the ingredients and knead by hand (mix first in a large bowl, then turn out and knead) or in a stand mixer fitted with the dough hook until the dough is elastic.

2. Cover the bowl with plastic wrap and let the dough rise until it has doubled in size, about 1 hour in a warm room.

3. Spray a 9 x 13-inch baking pan with baking spray.

4. Flour your work surface and turn out the dough. Divide the dough into 12 pieces and shape into rounds. Arrange the buns in the pan in 4 rows of 3 buns. Cover the pan with plastic wrap or put the pan in a large plastic bag and tie the end closed. Refrigerate overnight.

ON PREP DAY 2

1. Remove the pan from the refrigerator and heat the oven to 200°F. Remove the plastic and bake the buns for 1 hour 15 minutes. They will be fully baked though still pale.

2. Let the buns cool in the pan for a few minutes for easier handling, then transfer to a wire rack to cool. When the buns are completely cool, put them in a gallon-size zip-top plastic bag or wrap in plastic. If you plan on cooking the buns later in the day or the next day, you can leave the buns at room temperature; otherwise, refrigerate the buns for a few days' storage or freeze for longer storage.

ON BAKING DAY

When you're ready to bake, heat the oven to 350°F and place the buns on a baking sheet. Bake for 15 minutes, or until richly browned. Frozen buns will take a few minutes more to bake.

BUTTER LAYERED BUNS

These buns are inspired by biscuits that have buttery layers between the dough.

The fun thing about buns like these is that they're a little unpredictable in the oven, so no two buns will look exactly the same. But they'll all have layers, and they'll all be soft on the inside, but with a little chew and a bit of crunch on the crust and edges.

MAKES 12 BUNS

ON PREP DAY

1. Combine all the ingredients except the olive oil and butter in a gallon-size plastic zip-top bag. Massage and squish the bag all over until the ingredients are thoroughly mixed and there are no dry bits left. The dough will stick to the bag.

2. Add the olive oil and massage the bag until all the dough is coated with oil and it's no longer sticking to the bag. You're not trying to incorporate the oil into the dough, but simply coating the dough with the oil. Close the bag and refrigerate overnight or up to 24 hours.

ON BAKING DAY

1. Line a baking sheet with parchment paper.

2. Take the dough out of the refrigerator, heat the oven to 350°, generously flour your work surface, and turn out the dough. Don't be alarmed—the dough will spread a bit on your work surface. Fold the left and right sides of the dough to the center and press down to secure it. Fold the top and bottom of the dough to the center and press down to secure. You should have a rough square of dough.

3. Using a rolling pin, roll the dough to approximately 12 inches square. Spread the softened butter evenly over the surface of the dough.

4. Fold the dough in thirds from top down, then bottom up, like a fat tri-fold wallet. Fold in the same way, left and right.

5. Roll the dough into a rectangle approximately 7 x 10 inches. Using a sharp knife or pizza cutter, cut it into thirds to make three 10-inch strips. Cut each strip into 4 pieces for a total of 12 squares (about 2 1/2 inches).

6. Place the squares on the prepared baking sheet, leaving room between them to rise. Cover the pan with plastic wrap and set aside to rise for 30 minutes. The squares might not be doubled in size after rising, but they should feel soft and puffy if you poke one lightly with a fingertip.

7. Remove the plastic and bake the buns until they are golden-brown and the internal temperature is 195°F on an instant-read thermometer, about 25 minutes. Cool on a wire rack.

2 1/2 cups (11 1/4 ounces) bread flour, plus more as needed

1/4 cup instant mashed potatoes

1 teaspoon instant yeast

1 teaspoon kosher salt

1 tablespoon sugar

1 1/2 cups room temperature water

2 tablespoons olive oil

2 tablespoons unsalted butter, softened

SWEET BUTTER BUNS

Sweet, buttery, and just a bit decadent, these buns are great for breakfast or brunch, but they also pair well with spicy food.

The butter in the center of the bun melts into the dough surrounding it, creating a little sweet-salty-buttery surprise. And if it seems odd to use unsalted butter but then add salt, there's a reason for it: This way, you will encounter small pockets of saltiness, waking up your taste buds, instead of having evenly salted buns, where you don't really taste the salt.

MAKES 12 BUNS

ON PREP DAY

1. Spray a 9 x 13-inch baking pan with baking spray.

2. Combine all the dough ingredients in a stand mixer and knead with the dough hook until smooth. You can also mix the ingredients in a large bowl, using a hand-held electric mixer, then knead by hand. Cover the bowl with plastic wrap and set aside to rise until the dough has doubled in size, about 1 hour.

3. Meanwhile, combine the butter center ingredients in a small bowl. Mix until just combined—you're not looking to dissolve the sugar.

4. Flour your work surface and turn out the dough. Divide it into 12 equal pieces and form each into a flat disk about 3 inches in diameter. Place a teaspoon of the butter-sugar mixture on the center of each disk. Working with one disk at a time, stretch the edges of the dough, pulling them up and then over top of the butter center to enclose the butter; pinch to seal. Place the bun, seam side down, in the prepared pan. Continue with the rest of the buns.

5. Cover the pan with plastic wrap and refrigerate overnight or up to 24 hours.

ON BAKING DAY

1. Take the pan out of the refrigerator and heat the oven to 350°F.

2. Remove the plastic and bake the buns until nicely browned and the internal temperature is 190°F on an instant-read thermometer, about 25 minutes. Transfer the buns to a wire rack to cool.

Nonstick baking spray

FOR THE DOUGH

1 cup room temperature water

2¼ teaspoons active dry yeast

¼ cup sugar

3 cups (13½ ounces) bread flour, plus more as needed

1 teaspoon kosher salt

2 tablespoons unsalted butter

1 large egg

¼ cup nonfat dry milk

¼ cup (1½ ounces) semolina flour

FOR THE BUTTER CENTER

4 tablespoons unsalted butter, at room temperature

¼ teaspoon kosher salt

2 tablespoons Vanilla Sugar (recipe on p. 189)

TIP

You can use regular sugar instead of Vanilla Sugar, if you like, or try brown sugar or maple sugar for a sweeter option.

WHOLE WHEAT, WHITE, *and* RYE BUNS

Warm from the oven, it's hard to resist spreading these flavorful buns with a little butter. Or try them with Chive Cream Cheese (recipe on p. 181), or make mini ham sandwiches with mayonnaise and tomatoes.

If you have leftover buns, cut them into rustic chunks and toast them to make wonderful croutons for topping a salad or slice them thin and dry them in the oven to make crostini.

MAKES 12 BUNS

ON PREP DAY

1. Line a baking sheet with parchment paper or sprinkle with cornmeal.

2. Combine all the ingredients in a stand mixer and knead with the dough hook until smooth. You can also mix the ingredients in a large bowl, using a hand-held electric mixer, then knead by hand. Cover the bowl and set aside to rise until the dough has doubled in size, about an hour.

3. Flour your work surface and turn out the dough. Divide it into 12 equal pieces and roll each piece into a ball.

4. Arrange the balls on the prepared baking sheet and cover the sheet with plastic wrap or place it in a large plastic bag and tie the open end closed. Refrigerate overnight or up to 24 hours.

ON BAKING DAY

1. Take the pan out of the refrigerator and heat the oven to 350°F.

2. Remove the plastic and bake the buns until they're nicely browned and the internal temperature is 205°F on an instant-read thermometer, about 25 minutes. Remove the buns from the pan and cool on a rack.

Cornmeal, for the pan (optional)

1½ cups room temperature water

2¼ teaspoons active dry yeast

1 tablespoon sugar

1 cup (4½ ounces) rye flour

1½ cups (6¾ ounces) whole wheat flour

1½ cups (6¾ ounces) bread flour, plus more as needed

1½ teaspoons kosher salt

2 tablespoons olive oil

1 tablespoon caraway seeds

2 tablespoons sesame seeds

TIP

Since these buns are baked on a large baking sheet with room between them, they spread and flatten a bit, which makes them perfect for small sandwiches. If you prefer a taller, rounder bun, bake them in a 9 x 13-inch pan.

HONEY-POTATO BUNS

Who needs toast at breakfast when you can have a basket full of soft, fluffy buns? These buns are perfect for sopping up runny egg yolks or for making an on-the-go breakfast sandwich. But they aren't just for breakfast—they're just as good for lunch or dinner.

Semolina flour adds depth of flavor while instant potatoes create fluffiness.

MAKES 24 BUNS

ON PREP DAY

1. Combine the water, honey, yeast, bread flour, semolina flour, dry milk, and potato flakes in a stand mixer fitted with the dough hook. Knead until the dough is smooth and elastic.

2. Add the salt and butter and continue kneading until they are completely incorporated and the dough is smooth, shiny, and elastic.

3. Cover the bowl with plastic wrap and set aside for 45 minutes. Meanwhile, line a rimmed half-sheet baking pan with parchment paper.

4. Flour your work surface and turn out the dough. Divide it into 24 equal pieces and roll each piece into a ball. Arrange the balls on the prepared baking pan, and sprinkle the tops with rice flour. If you don't have rice flour, you can use bread or all-purpose flour—this keeps the plastic from sticking to the top of the buns.

5. Cover the pan with plastic wrap or place the whole pan in a large plastic bag and tie the open end shut. Refrigerate overnight or up to 24 hours.

ON BAKING DAY

1. Take the pan out of the refrigerator and heat the oven to 350°F.

2. Remove the plastic and bake the buns until nicely browned and the internal temperature registers 195°F on an instant-read thermometer, about 25 minutes. Transfer to a wire rack to cool.

1½ cups room temperature water

2 tablespoons honey

1 teaspoon instant yeast

3 cups (13½ ounces) bread flour, plus more as needed

½ cup (3 ounces) semolina flour

¼ cup nonfat dry milk

¼ cup instant potato flakes

1½ teaspoons kosher salt

2 tablespoons unsalted butter, at room temperature

White rice flour (optional)

TIP

No stand mixer? No problem. Combine all the ingredients in a large bowl, leave out about ½ cup of the bread flour and the white rice flour. When the ingredients are thoroughly mixed, sprinkle some of the reserved bread flour on your work surface and knead the dough by hand, adding flour as needed to keep it from sticking, until the dough is smooth and elastic.

BUTTERMILK ROLLS

Some people assume that buttermilk contains a lot of butter (translation, fat), but it doesn't.

In the old days, buttermilk was the liquid left over after butter was made from cream. These days, buttermilk is a thick, cultured product, but it's still a lower-fat option. You can even buy nonfat buttermilk. It adds a nice tangy flavor to this bread—not sour, but with a little more character than a typical white bun.

MAKES 12 ROLLS

ON PREP DAY

1. Line a baking sheet with parchment paper or sprinkle with cornmeal.

2. Combine all the ingredients in a stand mixer and knead with the dough hook until smooth. You can also mix the ingredients in a large bowl, then knead by hand.

3. Cover the bowl and set aside to rise until the dough has doubled in size, about 1 hour.

4. Flour your work surface and turn out the dough. Divide it into 12 equal pieces and roll each piece into a ball.

5. Arrange the balls on the prepared baking pan and cover it with plastic wrap or place it in a large plastic bag and tie the open end closed. Refrigerate overnight or up to 24 hours.

ON BAKING DAY

1. Take the dough out of the refrigerator and heat the oven to 350°F.

2. Remove the plastic and bake the buns until nicely browned and the internal temperature reaches 195°F on an instant-read thermometer, about 25 minutes. Transfer the buns to a wire rack and let cool.

Cornmeal, for the pan (optional)

$1\frac{1}{2}$ cups buttermilk, at room temperature

2 tablespoons sugar

$2\frac{1}{4}$ teaspoons active dry yeast

3 cups ($13\frac{1}{2}$ ounces) bread flour, plus more as needed

1 teaspoon kosher salt

$\frac{1}{2}$ cup instant mashed potato flakes

2 tablespoons unsalted butter

TIP

If you don't use buttermilk often, you can buy powdered buttermilk and mix it with water according to the package directions. It's not exactly the same, but it's close enough for most baking applications.

HAMBURGER *and* HOT DOG BUNS

I'll admit it—I don't always make my own hamburger and hot dog buns. But having grown up in Chicago, I like hot dog buns topped with poppy seeds, and they're hard to find where I live now. It's easier to make them than to find them at the market.

Another good reason for making buns is that hot dogs and burgers come in a variety of sizes, but buns are pretty standard. It's nice to make buns to fit their contents.

MAKES 12 BUNS

ON PREP DAY

1. Line a baking sheet with parchment paper or sprinkle with cornmeal.

2. Combine all the ingredients except the egg wash and seeds in a stand mixer and knead with the dough hook until smooth. You can also mix the ingredients in a large bowl using a hand-held electric mixer, then knead by hand.

3. Cover the bowl with plastic wrap and set aside to rise until the dough has doubled in size, about 1 hour.

4. Flour your work surface and turn out the dough. Divide it into 12 equal pieces and roll each piece into a ball.

5. For hamburger buns, flatten the balls into disks, then push and stretch them so they're about 4 inches in diameter. You want to work them so the center is thinner and the outer edge is thicker. This way, when the dough rises in the center, it will form a flatter top. If you form the buns into an evenly thick disk, the center of the bun will rise more than the edges, and you'll end up with something that looks more like a fat dinner roll than a burger bun. For hot dog buns, roll the dough pieces on your work surface as a child would form a snake from clay, until you have an evenly thick rope about 6 inches long.

6. Arrange the dough pieces on the prepared baking pan, leaving room between them to rise. If you prefer buns that touch each other, like commercial buns, then place the buns close together on the sheet, leaving an inch or less of space. Cover the pan with plastic wrap or place it in a large plastic bag and tie the open end closed. Refrigerate overnight or up to 24 hours.

ON BAKING DAY

1. Take the dough out of the refrigerator and heat the oven to 350°F.

2. Remove the plastic and brush the dough with egg wash. Sprinkle the burger buns with sesame seeds and the hot dog buns with poppyseeds, if desired. Bake the buns until nicely browned and the internal temperature is 195°F on an instant-read thermometer, about 25 minutes. Transfer the buns to a wire rack to cool.

Cornmeal, for the pan (optional)

1 1/2 cups room temperature water

2 1/4 teaspoons active dry yeast

1/4 cup nonfat dry milk

2 tablespoons sugar

3 1/2 cups (5 3/4 ounces) bread flour, plus more as needed

1 1/2 teaspoons kosher salt

2 tablespoons unsalted butter

Egg wash (1 large egg beaten with 1 tablespoon water)

Sesame seeds and poppyseeds (optional)

TIP

My rule of thumb for making buns for hot dogs and other sausage shapes is to form the dough into a log that's about the same size as the hot dog. When the dough expands during rising and baking, it will be just about perfect to enclose the hot dog with enough extra space for the fillings.

SLIDER BUNS

These small buns are perfect for small burgers or mini pulled pork sandwiches, but they can also be used for almost anything, really— dinner rolls, breakfast sandwiches (with a pork sausage patty, cheese and egg or with ham and egg), or a snack, slathered with peanut butter and jelly.

MAKES 12 BUNS

ON PREP DAY

1. Spray a 9 x 13-inch baking pan with baking spray.

2. Combine all the ingredients in a stand mixer and knead with the dough hook until smooth. You can also mix the ingredients in a large bowl, using a hand-held electric mixer, then knead by hand. Cover the bowl with plastic wrap and set aside to rise until the dough has doubled in size, about 1 hour.

3. Flour your work surface and turn out the dough. Divide it into 12 equal pieces and roll each piece into a ball.

4. Arrange the balls on the prepared baking pan, then flatten each one, pressing down in the center more than at the edges. Cover the pan with plastic wrap or place it in a large plastic bag and tie the open end closed and refrigerate overnight or up to 24 hours.

ON BAKING DAY

1. Take the pan out of the refrigerator and heat the oven to 350°F.

2. Remove the plastic and bake the buns until nicely browned and the internal temperature reaches 195°F on an instant-read thermometer, about 20 minutes. Transfer the buns to a wire rack and let cool.

Nonstick baking spray

1 cup room temperature water

2¼ teaspoons active dry yeast

½ cup instant mashed potato flakes

2 cups (9 ounces) bread flour, plus more as needed

2 tablespoons sugar

1 teaspoon kosher salt

1 tablespoon olive oil

TIP

If you like, before baking, brush the buns with an egg wash and sprinkle with poppyseeds, sesame seeds, or both.

CRISPY RYE BREADSTICKS

Crisp breadsticks are addictive, and since they're dry, they have a long storage life—if they last that long. This makes them a great make-ahead dish for a dinner party or holiday.

If you don't like caraway seeds, or if you're not sure about your guests' preferences, you can omit them.

MAKES ABOUT 70 BREADSTICKS

ON PREP DAY

Mix together all of the ingredients, except the 1 teaspoon of oil, in a medium bowl until well combined. Drizzle the remaining teaspoon of oil into a zip-top bag, place the dough in the bag, and massage the dough to coat it with oil. Seal the bag and refrigerate.

ON BAKING DAY

1. Heat the oven to 350°F and line two baking sheets with parchment paper.

2. Flour your work surface, turn out the dough, and divide it in half. Using a rolling pin, roll half of the dough into a rectangle about 8 x 14 inches. Using a pizza cutter, pastry cutter, or sharp knife, cut strips about ⅜ inch wide by 8 inches long. You should have about 35 strips. Roll out the other half of the dough and cut strips in the same way.

3. Transfer the dough strips to the baking sheets. They will stretch as you move them, which is fine.

4. Bake each sheet as you fill it until the breadsticks are lightly browned and crisp, about 15 minutes. Transfer the breadsticks to a rack to cool completely.

1 cup room temperature water

1 teaspoon active dry yeast

1 cup (4½ ounces) medium rye flour

1½ cups (6¾ ounces) bread flour, plus more as needed

1 teaspoon kosher salt

2 teaspoons sugar

2 tablespoons olive oil, plus 1 teaspoon for the bag

2 teaspoons caraway seeds

TIP

Twist and shape the breadsticks before baking for a fun look.

CHEESY BREADSTICK TWISTS

These fat, soft, cheesy breadsticks get their flavor from Cheddar cheese powder and grated Parmesan. If you've never used Cheddar cheese powder, it's worth seeking out. It's great in sauces, in breads, and sprinkled on vegetables.

Look for powdered cheese products that are dried and don't have added salt or flavorings. The artificial cheese-flavored orange powder that's sold for sprinkling on popcorn is likely to have a much higher percentage of salt and would make recipes like this way too salty and not cheesy enough.

For the Parmesan, use the good stuff (imported) if you have it (the flavor will be more intense), though the domestic cheese is fine too.

MAKES 12 BREADSTICKS

2½ cups (11¼ ounces) unbleached all-purpose flour, plus more as needed
¼ cup Cheddar cheese powder
1 teaspoon instant yeast
½ teaspoon kosher salt
1 cup room temperature water
1 tablespoon sugar
2 tablespoons olive oil, divided
1 cup grated Parmesan cheese

ON PREP DAY

1. Combine the flour, cheese powder, yeast, salt, water, sugar, and 1 tablespoon olive oil and knead by hand (mix first in a large bowl, then turn out and knead) or in a stand mixer fitted with the dough hook, until the dough comes together cohesively—it doesn't need to be smooth or elastic.

2. Drizzle the remaining 1 tablespoon oil into a gallon-size zip-top plastic bag and transfer the dough to the bag. Squeeze and massage the bag to coat the dough with oil. Close the bag and refrigerate overnight or up to 24 hours.

ON BAKING DAY

1. Heat the oven to 350°F and line two baking sheets with parchment paper.

2. Flour your work surface lightly and turn out the dough. Pat the dough into a rough square shape, then use a rolling pin to roll it to approximately 8 x 12 inches.

3. Sprinkle the Parmesan over the top of the dough, then gently press the cheese into the dough with the rolling pin. Fold the dough in half lengthwise to form a 4 x 12-inch rectangle, then use the rolling pin to roll the dough to approximately 6 x 12 inches.

4. Using a sharp knife, pizza wheel, or pastry cutter, cut the dough into twelve 6-inch-long pieces. One at a time, transfer the pieces to the baking sheets, placing 6 on each pan with space between for rising. Stretch the dough to 9 to 10 inches long and twist them to form a spiral shape. If they begin to untwist a bit, that's okay. Just carry on until all dough pieces have been transferred and twisted, then

retwist any that need to be fixed—the gluten will have relaxed a bit and they'll be more willing to stay put. Gather up any cheese that might have spilled out of the breadsticks and sprinkle it on top.

5. Bake the breadsticks until they're nicely browned (yes, it's correct that there's no rise before baking), 25 to 35 minutes, rotating the pans about halfway through baking. Transfer the baked breadsticks to a rack to cool.

CRISP SESAME BREADSTICKS

These crisp breadsticks are crazy good, and they're simple to make. Unlike some breadsticks that have sesame seeds on the outside, these have the seeds inside the dough. You get all the flavor with much less bother and the seeds won't fall off.

If it seems odd to cut the breadsticks and bake immediately, don't worry about it—there's enough air in the dough to provide the perfect crisp texture.

MAKES 12 DOZEN BREADSTICKS

1 cup room temperature water

3 cups ($13^{1}/_{2}$ ounces) flour, plus more as needed

1 teaspoon kosher salt

$2^{1}/_{4}$ teaspoons active dry yeast

1 tablespoon sugar

2 tablespoons olive oil, plus a small amount for drizzling into the bag

$^{1}/_{4}$ cup toasted sesame seeds

ON PREP DAY

1. Combine all of the ingredients and knead by hand (mix first in a large bowl, then turn out and knead) or in a stand mixer fitted with the dough hook, until the dough is barely elastic.

2. Drizzle a small amount of oil into a gallon-size zip-top plastic bag and transfer the dough to the bag. Squish the bag to make sure the dough is thoroughly coated with the oil, then close the bag and refrigerate overnight.

ON BAKING DAY

1. Remove the dough from the refrigerator and heat the oven to 325°F. Line several baking sheets with parchment paper.

2. Flour your work surface lightly and turn out the dough. Divide it into 2 pieces. Working with one piece at a time, roll the dough to a 9 x 18-inch rectangle. With a sharp knife, pizza cutter, or pastry cutter, cut the dough into $^{1}/_{4}$-inch slices that are 9 inches long.

3. Transfer the dough strips to the baking sheets. They will stretch as you move them, which is fine. If you handle them carefully, you can keep them from stretching longer than the width of the pan, or allow them to stretch longer and then create hooks or spirals on the ends of the breadsticks.

4. Bake each sheet as you fill it for 12 to 15 minutes, or until the breadsticks are browned. If you're baking more than one pan at a time, rotate the pans halfway through baking so the breadsticks cook evenly—those at the bottom of the oven will cook much faster on the underside, so you might want to turn them over for the last few minutes of baking.

5. Remove the pans from the oven and transfer the breadsticks to a rack to cool. Roll out the second piece of dough, cut into strips, and continue baking until you've used up all of the dough.

HOAGIE BUNS *with* SPROUTED WHEAT FLOUR

Sprouted wheat flour is fairly new in the marketplace. It's a whole grain product, but the difference between this and other wheat products is that the wheat is allowed to begin sprouting before it is turned into flour. The health theory is that your body treats this sprouted wheat as a plant substance rather than as a grain. Whether that's true or not is another discussion, but the reason I like it is that it adds a lovely sweetness to the bread.

Hoagie buns are more substantial than hot dog buns and are perfect for sausage and peppers or other hearty fillings.

MAKES 8 BUNS

ON PREP DAY

1. Line a baking sheet with parchment paper.

2. Combine all the ingredients in a stand mixer and knead with the dough hook until smooth. You can also mix the ingredients in a large bowl using a hand-held electric mixer, then knead by hand.

3. Cover the bowl with plastic wrap and set aside to rise until the dough has doubled in size, about 1 hour.

4. When the dough has doubled, flour your work surface and turn out the dough. Divide it into 8 equal pieces and roll each piece into a ball, then roll into sausage-shaped logs about 5 inches long.

5. Arrange the logs on the prepared baking pan; cover the pan with plastic wrap or place it in a large plastic bag and tie the open end closed. Refrigerate overnight or up to 24 hours.

ON BAKING DAY

1. Take the dough out of the refrigerator and heat the oven to 350°F.

2. Remove the plastic and bake the buns until they are nicely browned and the internal temperature is 195°F on an instant-read thermometer, about 20 minutes. Transfer the buns to a wire rack to cool.

1 cup room temperature water

$2^1/_4$ teaspoons active dry yeast

1 tablespoon sugar

1 cup ($4^1/_2$ ounces) sprouted wheat flour

2 cups (9 ounces) bread flour, plus more as needed

2 tablespoons olive oil

1 teaspoon kosher salt

TIP

If you can't find sprouted wheat flour, white wheat flour is a good substitute.

KAISER ROLLS

Kaiser rolls are as much about the shape as the recipe. Traditional rolls are formed by making a rope of dough, then tying a particular style of knot. Once you've mastered the technique, it's a fast, simple method. Even if you fumble and get the knots a little off-center, the buns will taste fine.

Another option, and one used for commercial kaiser rolls, is to use a stamp that cuts the familiar pattern into the dough.

MAKES 8 ROLLS

ON PREP DAY

1. Line a baking sheet with parchment paper or sprinkle with cornmeal.

2. Combine all the ingredients in a stand mixer and knead with the dough hook until smooth. You can also mix the ingredients in a large bowl, using a hand-held electric mixer, then knead by hand.

3. Cover the bowl with plastic wrap and set aside to rise until the dough has doubled in size, about 1 hour.

4. When the dough has doubled, divide it into 8 pieces, and form each into a rope about 12 inches long. Make sure the ropes are well-floured, which will make knotting easier and help to maintain the definition of the design.

5. Working with one rope at a time, tie a loose knot in the center of the rope, leaving a hole in the center about 2 inches wide. The hole doesn't need to be precise, but just be sure the knot isn't too tight. Take one of the long ends of the rope and loop it through the hole again. Do the same with the other long end. One will loop under the circle of dough and one will loop over. This will leave you with a nub of dough in the center. The loops around the outside should be as evenly spaced as you can manage.

6. Place the finished bun on the prepared baking sheet and continue making the rest of the rolls in the same way.

7. Cover the pan with plastic wrap or place it in a large plastic bag and tie the open end closed; refrigerate overnight or up to 24 hours

ON BAKING DAY

1. Take the dough out of the refrigerator and heat the oven to 350°F.

2. Remove the plastic and bake the rolls until they're nicely browned and the internal temperature is 195°F on an instant-read thermometer, about 20 minutes. Transfer the rolls to a wire rack and let cool.

Cornmeal, for the pan (optional)
1 cup room temperature water
1 large egg
1 teaspoon barley malt syrup
2¼ teaspoons active dry yeast
3 cups (13½ ounces) bread flour, plus more as needed
1 teaspoon kosher salt
2 tablespoons unsalted butter

TIP

Barley malt syrup adds a familiar flavor to many breads and buns, like these kaiser rolls. If you can't find barley malt syrup, try the malt powder that's used for making malted milk. I'm sure you can find uses for that.

GARLIC KNOTS

Garlic knots sound fancy, but they're actually pretty simple to make. The flavor goes well with a number of different cuisines, and the chives add a bit of visual interest to the buns.

MAKES 12 KNOTS

ON PREP DAY

1. Combine all of the ingredients and knead by hand (mix first in a large bowl, then turn out and knead) or in a stand mixer fitted with the dough hook until the dough is elastic.

2. Cover the bowl with plastic wrap and let the dough rise until it has doubled in size, about 1 hour in a warm room.

3. Meanwhile, line a baking sheet with parchment paper.

4. Turn out the dough onto a lightly floured work surface. Divide the dough into 12 equal pieces, then roll each piece into a rope about 10 inches long. There's no need to be fancy—just roll it as a child would roll a snake out of clay. Tie each rope into a simple loose knot—you're not making a noose or tying a ship to a dock. Place the finished knots on the prepared baking pan, leaving room between them to rise.

5. Cover the pan with plastic wrap and refrigerate overnight or up to 24 hours.

ON BAKING DAY

1. Take the pan out of the refrigerator and heat the oven to 350°F.

2. Remove the plastic and bake the buns until they're nicely browned and the internal temperature registers 195°F on an instant-read thermometer, about 35 minutes. Transfer the buns to a wire rack and let cool.

1 cup room temperature water

2¼ teaspoons active dry yeast

1 tablespoon sugar

3 cups (13½ ounces) bread flour, plus more as needed

1 tablespoon fresh or dried chives

2 tablespoons garlic olive oil

1 teaspoon kosher salt

TIP

I used to be opposed to flavored olive oils, thinking that if I wanted the flavor of garlic or citrus or herbs, I'd just add it to the dish and use plain oil. But recently I changed my mind.

Garlic oil, in particular, is handy to have around. The flavor is much mellower than fresh garlic, and it's a nice addition to a dipping oil, brushed on bread to make garlic toast, or incorporated into a salad dressing. Plus it will save you from reaching into the garlic keeper and finding nothing but skins and a few sprouted cloves.

Garlic olive oil used to be a specialty item, but these days most grocery stores stock it. The strength of the garlic flavor can vary from brand to brand, so taste before you use it on something delicate, like a salad.

SPELT DINNER ROLLS

Spelt is an ancient grain that is a species of wheat. Over the last couple of years, spelt flour has become more popular and more readily available in grocery stores. The whole grain version is easier to find than the more refined white version, and that's what I used here, but white spelt flour would also work.

Spelt contains gluten, but it behaves differently than the gluten in wheat flour, so for a foolproof recipe, I mixed spelt with wheat to get the advantages of both products.

MAKES 12 ROLLS

ON PREP DAY

1. Spray a 9 x 13-inch baking pan with baking spray.

2. Combine all the ingredients in a stand mixer and knead with the dough hook until smooth. You can also mix the ingredients in a large bowl, using a hand-held electric mixer or Danish dough hook, then finish kneading by hand. Cover the bowl with plastic wrap and set aside to rise until the dough has doubled in size, about 1 hour.

3. Flour your work surface and turn out the dough. Divide it into 12 equal pieces and roll each piece into a ball. Arrange the balls on the prepared baking pan and cover the pan with plastic wrap or place it in a large plastic bag and tie the open end closed. Refrigerate overnight or up to 24 hours.

ON BAKING DAY

1. Take the dough out of the refrigerator and heat the oven to 350°F.

2. Remove the plastic and bake the rolls until nicely browned and the internal temperature is 205°F on an instant-read thermometer, about 25 minutes. Cool the rolls on a rack.

Nonstick baking spray

1 cup room temperature water

2¼ teaspoons active dry yeast

2 tablespoons sugar

1½ cups (6¾ ounces) spelt flour

2 cups (9 ounces) bread flour, plus more as needed

2 tablespoons unsalted butter

1 teaspoon kosher salt

¼ cup nonfat dry milk

TIP

Spelt flour can be substituted for whole wheat flour or white wheat flour in many recipes. It's in the wheat family, but has a slightly different flavor, so it's good for variety. Try it in your favorite cookie in place of some of the white flour.

PAR-BAKED WHOLE WHEAT CLOVERLEAF ROLLS

Cloverleaf rolls are a fun shape, with three or four lobes that you can pull apart. I think the three-leaf version is more attractive, but the four-leaf version gives you more bits to pull apart—and some folks might think they're lucky. There's no reason you can't make some of each version.

MAKES 12 ROLLS

ON PREP DAY

1. Spray a 12-cup muffin pan with baking spray.

2. Combine all the ingredients in a stand mixer and knead with the dough hook until smooth. You can also mix the ingredients in a large bowl, using a hand-held electric mixer, then knead by hand. Cover the bowl with plastic wrap and set aside to rise until the dough has doubled in size, about 1 hour.

3. When the dough has doubled, turn it out onto a lightly floured work surface and divide into 12 pieces. Divide each of the 12 pieces into 3 or 4 pieces, depending on whether you want 3-leaf clovers or 4-leaf clovers. Roll each piece into a ball and place them in the wells of the prepared muffin pan, making sure that all 3 (or 4) are evenly snugged into the pan and touching the bottom of the muffin cup.

4. Cover the pan with plastic wrap or place it in a large plastic bag and tie the open end closed; set it aside until the dough has doubled in size and has risen above the top of the muffin cups, about 40 minutes.

5. While the dough is rising, heat the oven to 200°F.

6. When the dough has risen, remove the plastic and bake the rolls for 1 hour 15 minutes. The rolls will be cooked through but still pale.

7. Remove the rolls from the pan and let them cool completely on a rack. You can leave them at room temperature overnight, refrigerate for a few days, or freeze them for longer storage.

ON BAKING DAY

Heat the oven to 350°F. Place as many rolls as you want to bake on a baking sheet, leaving some space between them for even heating, and bake until they are nicely browned, about 15 minutes. Serve warm or at room temperature.

Nonstick baking spray
1 cup room temperature water
2¼ teaspoons instant yeast
1 tablespoon sugar
¼ cup nonfat dry milk
¾ cup (3⅜ ounces) whole wheat flour
2 cups bread flour, plus more as needed
1 teaspoon kosher salt
2 tablespoons unsalted butter

TIP

These rolls freeze very well after the first baking, so you can make them well in advance and have them ready whenever you need them, whether you're making a big batch for company or just a few rolls for a family dinner.

WHITE RYE SANDWICH BUNS
with NIGELLA SEED TOPPING

White rye flour isn't the same thing as light rye. The white rye is lighter and the flour is finer than most rye flours, but you can substitute light rye or any other rye flour if that's what you have. The buns won't be the same, but they'll still be good.

These buns are a little chewy, with a shiny crust from the egg wash. The nigella seeds add a little salty and peppery flavor as well as a pop of color. Nigella seeds are sometimes sold as charnushka and are often used in Indian cooking as well as on Jewish rye bread.

You could bake these as round buns, but I like them flattened so they can be used for sandwiches.

MAKES 8 BUNS

Nonstick baking spray

1 cup room temperature water

2¼ teaspoons active dry yeast

1 tablespoon sugar

1 cup (4½ ounces) white rye flour

2 cups (9 ounces) bread flour, plus more as needed

1 teaspoon kosher salt

2 tablespoons unsalted butter

Egg wash (1 large egg beaten with 1 tablespoon water)

2 tablespoons nigella seeds

ON PREP DAY

1. Combine all of the ingredients except the egg wash and nigella seeds. Knead by hand (mix first in a large bowl, then turn out and knead) or in a stand mixer fitted with the dough hook, until the dough is elastic.

2. Cover the bowl with plastic wrap and let the dough rise until it has doubled in size, about 1 hour in a warm room.

3. Meanwhile, line a baking sheet with parchment paper.

4. Flour your work surface, then turn out the dough and divide it into 8 pieces. Form the pieces into balls, then flatten them into disks about 3½ to 4 inches in diameter. You can do this easily by pressing and stretching the dough with your fingers. Put the disks on the pan, then cover the pan with plastic wrap or place the whole pan in a large plastic bag and tie the open end shut. Refrigerate overnight or up to 24 hours.

ON BAKING DAY

1. Remove the pan from the refrigerator and heat the oven to 350°F.

2. Remove the plastic, brush the buns with the egg wash, and sprinkle with the nigella seeds. Bake the buns until they're golden-brown and the internal temperature is 205°F on an instant-read thermometer, about 35 minutes.

3. Transfer the buns to a wire rack and cool.

MARBLED WHITE *and* RYE BUNS

Many marble recipes are actually tightly formed swirls. While this is a fine look, I wanted to have some fun with these buns and make them more randomly swirled, like actual marbles made from glass.

All the buns have about the same ratio of white to rye, but they look much different from each other.

MAKES 12 BUNS

ON PREP DAY

1. Spray a 9 x 13-inch baking pan with baking spray.

2. Combine the water, sugar, yeast, salt, olive oil, and 2 cups bread flour in a stand mixer or large bowl. Knead with the dough hook or stir with a wooden spoon until mixed well. You will have a very wet dough at this point.

3. Transfer half of the dough to a separate bowl and set it aside while you work on the first half. Add the remaining 1 cup of bread flour to the dough left in the stand mixer and knead until smooth. Transfer to a clean bowl, cover with plastic wrap, and set aside.

4. Transfer the reserved dough to the stand mixer (there's no need to wash it first) and add the dark rye flour. Knead the mixture with the dough hook until the dough is smooth. Cover the bowl with plastic wrap and set aside with the first bowl until the doughs have doubled in size, about 1 hour. It's fine if one dough rises faster than another; the important thing is that both doughs double in size.

5. When the doughs have doubled, flour your work surface and turn out the white dough. Pat it into a flat disk. Place the rye dough on top of the white dough and stretch and pat it so it evenly covers the white dough. Cut the combined dough disk into 12 even pieces.

6. Working with one piece of dough at a time, fold, twist, mash, and squeeze it as desired to make an interesting pattern of the two doughs. You're not trying to mix them, so don't get too carried away. Form the piece into a ball and place it on the prepared baking pan. Repeat with the remaining pieces of dough. Cover the pan with plastic wrap or place it in a large plastic bag and tie the open end closed; refrigerate overnight or up to 24 hours.

ON BAKING DAY

1. Take the pan out of the refrigerator and heat the oven to 350°F.

2. Remove the plastic and bake the buns until they're nicely browned and the internal temperature is 205°F on an instant-read thermometer, about 25 minutes. Transfer to a wire rack and let cool.

Nonstick baking spray

3/4 cup room temperature water

1 tablespoon sugar

1 1/2 teaspoons active dry yeast

1 teaspoon kosher salt

1 tablespoon olive oil

3 cups (13 1/2 ounces) bread flour, divided, plus more as needed

1 cup dark rye flour

TIP

Cocoa powder is often used to make rye bread darker. A teaspoon of cocoa powder added to the rye portion of the dough would make the color difference here even more dramatic. It's such a small amount that you won't notice any flavor difference.

CRESCENT ROLLS

Crescent rolls are the casual version of the much more complicated croissant. The form is the same, but the dough is much different. Crescents have significantly less fat, and they're much easier to make. Shaping them is good practice for making croissants, though.

I think one of the best things about crescent rolls is the way the tips brown just a little more than the rest of the buns, so you get that variation of browning from the tips to the tops, to the soft, fluffy interior.

MAKES 16 ROLLS

ON PREP DAY

1. Line a baking sheet with parchment paper.

2. Combine all the ingredients in a stand mixer and knead with the dough hook until smooth. You can also mix the ingredients in a large bowl, then knead by hand.

3. Cover the bowl and set aside to rise until the dough has doubled in size, about 1 hour.

4. When the dough has risen, lightly flour your work surface and turn out the dough. Divide it into two pieces.

5. Roll out the first piece into a circle about 5 inches in diameter, then cut it into eight even pie-shaped wedges. Working with one at a time, stretch the length of the wedge to 6 to 7 inches long and stretch the base to 5 inches wide. Starting at the base, roll up the dough, form a crescent-shaped curve, then place it on the prepared sheet, leaving space between the crescents for them to rise.

6. Continue with the second piece of dough, cutting wedges and shaping crescents. You might need a second baking sheet.

7. Cover the pan(s) with plastic wrap or place it in a large plastic bag and tie the open end closed. Refrigerate overnight or up to 24 hours.

ON BAKING DAY

1. Take the pan out of the refrigerator and heat the oven to 350°F.

2. Remove the plastic and bake the crescent rolls until nicely browned and the internal temperature is 195°F on an instant-read thermometer, about 20 minutes. Transfer the rolls to a wire rack and let cool.

1 cup room temperature water

1 tablespoon sugar

2 1/4 teaspoons active dry yeast

2 1/2 cups (11 1/4 ounces) bread flour, plus more as needed

1/2 cup instant mashed potato flakes

1 teaspoon kosher salt

1 large egg

1/4 cup nonfat dry milk

TIP

These crescents would be nice with an egg wash, which would create a shiny surface and add a little more crispness.

SOURDOUGH ENGLISH MUFFINS

There are a few ways to make English muffins: They can be made from a thick dough and cut and baked like biscuits; they can be made like flat buns; or they can be made with a batter, like a big, fat pancake. This is the batter version.

You'll need muffin rings to contain the batter while you cook the English muffins (look for 3½-inch rings, the standard English muffin size). If you don't want to buy muffin rings, you can use short, squat cans with the top and bottom removed. Tuna cans are often recommended, but many brands now use cans with formed bottoms that can't be removed with a can opener. But if you like canned water chestnuts, those cans work, too.

MAKES 6 ENGLISH MUFFINS

ON PREP DAY
Whisk all of the ingredients together in a large bowl, forming a relatively thin batter rather than a dough. (The batter will bubble and rise, so don't use a bowl that's too small.) Cover with plastic wrap and leave at room temperature overnight.

ON BAKING DAY
1. Heat a griddle (or large frying pan) on medium heat with 6 muffin rings arranged on the griddle. Spray or brush the insides of the rings with oil, and let them heat with the griddle.

2. When the griddle is hot, ladle or pour the batter into the rings, filling them to about ¼ inch below the top of the rings. Cover the griddle—a sheet pan turned upside down on top of the rings is perfect—and reduce the heat to medium low. Cook until the top of the batter is set and has started to pull away from the sides of the rings, about 8 minutes.

3. Use a small spatula to flip the muffins (and rings) over, cover the pan again, and cook for another 5 minutes. You should now be able to slip the muffins out of the rings. If some need encouragement, slide a thin knife around the insides of the rings, then remove the rings.

4. Continue cooking the muffins until they are cooked through and the top and bottom are lightly browned—a skewer or small knife inserted into a muffin should come out clean and if you lift a muffin, it should feel light for its size. It's actually okay if the muffins are still a little bit moist inside because they're not really done until they're toasted. But you don't want them to be wet or soggy.

5. Let the muffins cool completely on a rack.

½ cup (4 ounces) sourdough starter (see p. 9)

2 cups (9 ounces) unbleached all-purpose flour

1 teaspoon sugar

1 teaspoon kosher salt

1½ cups room temperature water

Olive oil spray

TIP
One thing that makes an English muffin an English muffin is the rough interior, so you don't want to slice them with a knife. Instead, use a fork to stab all the way around the muffin until you can pull it apart. You'll have a rough, craggy interior that will toast nicely.

Sourdough English Muffins with Wine Jam
(recipe on p. 193)

BUNS, ROLLS & BREADSTICKS 95

PAR-BAKED HERB *and* CHEESE BUNS

These buns are perfect for taking to a potluck or family gathering, where they can be tossed in the oven at the last minute for browning—that way you can have fresh buns with absolutely no work on the day you bake them.

Yellow cheese looks more attractive in the buns, but you can use white Cheddar, if you prefer. The cheesy bits on the outsides of the buns brown and crisp, like those bits of a grilled cheese sandwich that hit the hot pan, adding to the texture.

MAKES 12 BUNS

ON PREP DAY

1. Combine all of the ingredients except the cheese and knead by hand (mix first in a large bowl, then turn out and knead) or in a stand mixer fitted with the dough hook, until the dough is elastic. Add the cheese and continue kneading until the cheese is evenly distributed in the dough—it's fine if the cheese breaks up into smaller bits during the kneading.

2. Return the dough to the bowl, cover with plastic wrap, and let the dough rise until it has doubled in size, about 1 hour in a warm room.

3. Spray a 12-cup muffin pan with baking spray. Flour your work surface and turn out the dough. Divide the dough into 12 equal pieces and roll each piece into a ball. Place the balls in the muffin cups and cover the pan with plastic wrap or place the whole pan in a large plastic bag and tie the open end shut. Set the pan aside until the buns have risen about an inch over the top of the pan, about 30 minutes.

4. Meanwhile, heat the oven to 200°F.

5. When the buns have risen, remove the plastic and bake the buns for 1 hour 15 minutes. The buns will be baked through but should brown very little.

6. Let the buns cool for 5 minutes in the pan, then remove them from the pan and cool completely on a rack.

7. You can leave the par-baked buns at room temperature for a day or refrigerate them for a few days before baking. For longer storage freeze them. They thaw quickly, or bake them from frozen.

ON BAKING DAY

1. Heat the oven to 350°F (or, if you're cooking other things in the oven, the buns will be fine baked at a higher or lower temperature—we're just warming and browning the buns).

2. Place the buns on a baking sheet and bake until nicely browned, about 15 minutes. Serve warm or let cool.

1 cup room temperature water
2¼ teaspoons active dry yeast
1 tablespoon sugar
2½ cups (11¼ ounces) bread flour, plus more as needed
¼ cup nonfat dry milk
¼ cup instant potato flakes
2 teaspoons parsley flakes
½ teaspoon dried thyme
½ teaspoon marjoram
¼ teaspoon garlic powder
1 teaspoon kosher salt
2 tablespoons unsalted butter
4 ounces mild Cheddar cheese, cut into small dice
Nonstick baking spray

PECAN BUTTER CRESCENTS

These crescents are filled with a little dab of pecan butter that sits in the center as a surprise. If you can find a coarsely ground nut butter, it adds some nice texture. If you can't find pecan butter, you can make your own, leaving it as smooth or as chunky as you like (see the recipe for Nut or Seed Butter on p. 191).

These crescents are not butter-laden, flaky croissants; they are the bread version that is shaped in the same way—and are as equally delicious.

MAKES 16 CRESCENTS

ON PREP DAY

1. Combine the water, yeast, sugar, flour, salt, and olive oil in a stand mixer and knead with the dough hook until the dough is smooth and elastic. Cover the bowl with plastic wrap and set aside for 45 minutes.

2. Line two baking sheets or four half-sheet baking pans with parchment paper.

3. Flour your work surface and turn out the dough. Knead it briefly by hand, then divide it in half. Roll one piece of dough into a 4 x 8-inch rectangle. Cut the rectangle in half so you have two 4 x 4-inch squares. Cut each square diagonally into quarters.

4. Working with one quarter at a time, and with the base of the triangle (what used to be the edge of the square) facing away from you, pull and stretch the point across from the base so that the distance between the two is about 6 inches. Grab the base of the triangle and pull to stretch the triangle another inch wider.

5. Put about 1 teaspoon of the pecan butter in the center of the very bottom of the triangle. Using a pastry brush, brush butter on the dough below that dollop of pecan butter.

6. Starting at the base of the triangle, roll the dough toward the tip of the triangle. Once the triangle is rolled, turn down the tips to form a crescent shape, then place the crescent on one of the prepared baking sheets.

7. Continue filling and rolling the crescents.

8. As each baking sheet is filled, cover the pans with plastic wrap or put the pan in a large plastic bag and tie the end closed. Refrigerate overnight.

ON BAKING DAY

1. Remove the pans from the refrigerator and heat the oven to 325°F.

2. Remove the plastic and bake the crescents until they are nicely browned and the internal temperature (in the dough, not in the filling) is 195°F on an instant-read thermometer, about 25 minutes. Cool the rolls on a wire rack.

1 cup lukewarm water

1 teaspoon instant yeast

2 tablespoons sugar

2½ cups (11¼ ounces) unbleached all-purpose flour, plus more as needed

1 teaspoon kosher salt

1 tablespoon olive oil

¼ cup pecan butter (preferably coarsely ground)

2 tablespoons unsalted butter, softened to a brushable consistency

TIP

If you're not a fan of nuts, replace them with chopped dried fruits in the center—apricots would be lovely. For something more savory, use chopped sun-dried tomatoes mixed with feta cheese.

OATMEAL *and* ORANGE BUNS *with* TOASTED COCONUT

These sweet buns will take you straight to the tropics, with their sunny orange flavor and toasty coconut.

To get the most orange juice flavor, I used frozen orange juice concentrate. A larger quantity of fresh orange juice to get the same flavor would change the yeast's function.

If you want more sweetness, more orange, and more coconut, make a simple confectioners' sugar icing with 2 cups of confectioners' sugar, a few drops of orange oil, and enough water—a teaspoon at a time—to make a thick but pourable icing. Drizzle the icing onto the buns when they're just slightly warm but not hot. Then sprinkle more toasted coconut on top.

MAKES 12 BUNS

ON PREP DAY

1. Spray a 9 x 13-inch baking pan with baking spray.

2. Combine all the ingredients in a stand mixer and knead with the dough hook until smooth. You can also mix the ingredients in a large bowl, using a hand-held electric mixer, then knead by hand. Cover the bowl with plastic wrap and set aside to rise until the dough has doubled in size, about 1 hour.

3. Flour your work surface and turn out the dough. Divide it into 12 equal pieces and roll each piece into a ball. Arrange the balls in the prepared pan and cover the pan with plastic wrap. Refrigerate overnight or up to 24 hours.

ON BAKING DAY

1. Take the dough out of the refrigerator and heat the oven to 350°F.

2. Remove the plastic and bake the buns until nicely browned and the internal temperature is 190°F on an instant-read thermometer, about 30 minutes. Remove the buns from the pan and cool on a rack.

Nonstick baking spray

$3/4$ cup room temperature water

$1/4$ cup frozen orange juice concentrate

$2 1/4$ teaspoons active dry yeast

2 tablespoons honey

1 cup oatmeal

$2 1/2$ cups ($11 1/4$ ounces) bread flour, plus more as needed

$1 1/2$ teaspoons kosher salt

2 ounces cream cheese, at room temperature

$1/4$ cup unsweetened coconut flakes, toasted

TIP

The rising time on these buns can be a little tricky depending on the orange juice concentrate. You might find that dough rises unexpectedly fast or that it takes its time. If the rise is fast, you can simply form the buns sooner. If the rise is slow, move the dough to a warm spot to encourage it. The important thing is that the dough needs to double in size for the first rise.

CHOCOLATE BUNS

Chocolate buns might sound a little odd, but chocolate bread is quite tasty for breakfast or brunch, particularly with a slather of butter or a smear of peanut butter.

These are sweet buns, but they aren't a super-sweet dessert—they're still a bread, not a cake. But if you wanted to slice them and layer them with some whipped cream and sliced fresh strawberries—well, I wouldn't stop you.

The chocolate chips increase the chocolate flavor as well as the sweetness, but you could use butterscotch chips, white chocolate chips, or peanut butter chips instead, if you like.

MAKES 12 BUNS

1 cup room temperature water
$1/4$ cup sugar
$1/4$ cup cocoa powder
$2^{1}/_2$ cups ($11^{1}/_4$ ounces) bread flour, plus more as needed
$2^{1}/_4$ teaspoons active dry yeast
2 tablespoons unsalted butter
1 teaspoon kosher salt
$1/4$ cup mini chocolate chips
Nonstick baking spray

ON PREP DAY

1. Combine all of the ingredients except the chocolate chips and knead by hand (mix first in a large bowl, then turn out and knead) or in a stand mixer fitted with the dough hook until the dough is elastic. Add the chocolate chips and continue kneading until the chips are evenly distributed in the dough.

2. Cover the bowl with plastic wrap and let the dough rise until it has doubled in size, about 1 hour in a warm room.

3. Spray a 12-cup muffin pan with baking spray. Flour your work surface and turn out the dough. Divide the dough into 12 equal pieces and roll each piece into a ball. Place the balls in the muffin cups, cover the pan with plastic wrap, and refrigerate overnight or up to 24 hours.

ON BAKING DAY

1. Take the pan out of the refrigerator and heat the oven to 350°F.

2. Remove the plastic from the pan and bake the buns until they are browned (it's a little hard to tell, since they're so dark to begin with, but you should see browning) and the internal temperature is 190°F on an instant-read thermometer, about 30 minutes. Let the buns cool in the pan for 5 minutes, then remove them and cool on a rack.

NUTELLA SWIRL ROLLS

There was a time when Nutella was the only chocolate-hazelnut spread on the market, but now there are several brands to choose from. Some are slightly thicker than others, so if the one you have is too thick to spread easily, warm it slightly in the microwave but don't let it get hot.

These buns have a tight spiral of light-colored bread with dark chocolate swirl. If you want to gild the lily, add a drizzle of confectioners' sugar icing—just mix a cup of confectioners' sugar with water, a few drops at a time, until the sugar is thin enough to drizzle over the buns. You won't need much; these buns are plenty sweet.

MAKES 12 ROLLS

ON PREP DAY

1. Combine the water, yeast, flour, sugar, salt, and hazelnut meal and knead by hand (mix first in a large bowl, then turn out and knead) or in a stand mixer fitted with the dough hook until the dough is elastic.

2. Cover the bowl with plastic wrap and let the dough rise until it has doubled in size, about 1 hour in a warm room.

3. Spray a 9 x 13-inch baking pan with baking spray.

4. When the dough has risen, flour your work surface and turn out the dough. Pat it into a rough square shape, then use a rolling pin to roll it to about 16 x 24 inches.

5. Spread the Nutella on the dough in as even a layer as possible. It's easiest to dollop on the Nutella, then spread it in that area rather than trying to spread it all from one large blob. Leave about an inch of the dough uncovered on one of the short ends.

6. Starting at the short end with the Nutella spread to the edge, roll the dough jellyroll style, leaving it a bit loose.

7. Cut the roll into 12 even pieces and arrange them, flat side up, in the prepared baking pan. Cover the pan with plastic wrap or place the whole pan in a large plastic bag and tie the open end closed. Refrigerate overnight or up to 24 hours.

ON BAKING DAY

1. Take the pan out of the refrigerator and heat the oven to 325°F.

2. Remove the plastic from the pan and bake the buns until they are golden-brown, about 40 minutes, or until an instant-read thermometer registers 195°F (make sure the thermometer is in the dough, not the filling). Let the buns cool in the pan for 10 minutes, then transfer them to a wire rack and let cool.

1 cup room temperature water
2¼ teaspoons active dry yeast
2½ cups (11¼ ounces) bread flour, plus more as needed
2 tablespoons sugar
1 teaspoon kosher salt
½ cup hazelnut meal
Nonstick baking spray
1 cup (8 ounces) Nutella®

TIP

If you can't find hazelnut meal, make your own: Grind skinned hazelnuts until they're the texture of coarse sand.

STRAWBERRY ROLLS *with* WALNUT SWIRL

These rolls are a pretty pink with a nutty swirl. How sweet these buns are depends a lot on how sweet and ripe the berries are.

If berries aren't in season or the berries at the store don't look appealing, use frozen berries. While frozen berries wouldn't be my first choice for something like a strawberry shortcake, they're perfectly fine for baking.

During the kneading, the berries get broken into smaller bits, so the final dough is filled with berry flavor, and there are just a few small berry pieces.

MAKES 12 ROLLS

ON PREP DAY

1. Make the filling: Combine the walnuts, sugar, and butter in a small bowl. Mix well and set aside until needed.

2. Make the dough: Spray a 9 x 13-inch baking pan with baking spray.

3. Combine all the dough ingredients in a stand mixer and knead with the dough hook until smooth. You can also mix the ingredients in a large bowl, using a hand-held electric mixer, then knead by hand. Cover the bowl with plastic wrap and set aside to rise until the dough has doubled in size, about 1 hour.

4. Flour your work surface lightly. Use a rolling pin to roll the dough into a 12-inch square. Sprinkle the filling over the top of the dough, leaving $1/2$ inch at the far side of the dough uncovered. Starting at the side closest to you, roll up the dough jellyroll style and pinch the seam closed.

5. Cut the dough into 12 pieces and place them, flat side down, in the prepared pan. Cover the pan with plastic wrap and refrigerate overnight or up to 24 hours.

ON BAKING DAY

1. Take the pan out of the refrigerator and heat the oven to 350°F.

2. Remove the plastic and bake the rolls until they're nicely browned and the internal temperature is 190°F on an instant-read thermometer (make sure you're in the dough and not in the filling), about 30 minutes. Transfer the rolls to a wire rack to cool.

FOR THE FILLING

1 cup (about 4 ounces) finely chopped walnuts

$1/2$ cup brown sugar

2 tablespoons unsalted butter, at room temperature

FOR THE DOUGH

Nonstick baking spray

1 cup (about 4 ounces) strawberries, diced

1 large egg

$3/4$ cup room temperature water

$2 1/4$ teaspoons active dry yeast

2 tablespoons sugar

3 cups ($13 1/2$ ounces) bread flour, plus more as needed

$1 1/2$ teaspoons kosher salt

4 tablespoons unsalted butter

$1/2$ cup instant mashed potato flakes

$1/4$ nonfat dry milk

TIP

These rolls are also good without the nut swirl. Just omit the nuts, and form the rolls into rounds. If you want to dress them up a bit, sprinkle with confectioners' sugar.

ALMOND ROLLS

These sweet buns have almond flavoring in the dough and a swirl of almond paste for even more sweet almond flavor. Almond paste is different from almond filling and is generally easy to find.

The almond paste can be a bit brittle when you roll it out, but don't worry if it breaks apart—just arrange it on top of the dough as evenly as possible.

MAKES 12 ROLLS

ON PREP DAY

1. Spray a 9 x 13-inch baking pan with baking spray.

2. Combine all the ingredients except the almond paste in a stand mixer and knead with the dough hook until smooth. You can also mix the ingredients in a large bowl, using a hand-held electric mixer, then knead by hand. Cover the bowl and set aside to rise until the dough has doubled in size, about 1 hour.

3. Flour your work surface lightly. Use a rolling pin to roll out the dough to form a 10-inch square. Roll out the almond paste to form a 10-inch square. Place the almond paste on top of the dough. If it cracks or breaks, simply arrange the almond paste on top of the dough as evenly as possible. Starting at the side closest to you, roll up the dough jellyroll style, and pinch the seam closed.

4. Cut the roll into 12 pieces. Pick the prettiest side to be the top. On the bottom, stretch and pinch the outer portion of the dough to cover the bottom and seal in the almond paste, which will burn if it contacts the bottom of the pan.

5. Place the buns, top side up, in the prepared pan. Cover the pan with plastic wrap or place it in a large plastic bag and tie the open end closed. Refrigerate overnight or up to 24 hours.

ON BAKING DAY

1. Take the pan out of the refrigerator while you heat your oven to 325°F.

2. Remove the plastic and bake the rolls until they're nicely browned on top and the internal temperature is 190°F on an instant-read thermometer, about 30 minutes. Transfer the rolls to a rack to cool.

Nonstick baking spray

1 cup room temperature water

1 large egg

2¼ teaspoons active dry yeast

¼ cup buttermilk powder

¼ cup sugar

3½ cups (15¾ ounces) bread flour, plus more as needed

4 tablespoons unsalted butter

1 teaspoon kosher salt

1 tablespoon pure vanilla extract

1 teaspoon almond extract

7 ounces almond paste

TIP

If it's easier, you can chop the almond paste into bits and spread it on top of the dough. For an even nuttier version, chop ¼ to ½ cup of almonds and sprinkle that on top of the almond paste.

STICKY BUNS

After all the loaves, buns, and flatbreads that have come out of my oven, I've gotten used to having fresh bread around. Most of the time, when I make a batch of buns, I'm more than happy to share. But these I hoard!

The graham cracker crumbs in the filling are an interesting little trick. They give the filling more body without the need for a huge amount of sugar. So while these are plenty sweet, thanks to that buttery-sugary-nutty topping (sometimes you just have to go wild!), there's still some restraint.

MAKES 12 BUNS

ON PREP DAY

1. Spray a 9 x 13-inch baking pan with baking spray.

2. Make the topping: In a medium saucepan, melt the butter over medium heat, then add the brown sugar and salt. Cook until the sugar melts, then turn off the heat and mix in the vanilla and heavy cream. Pour this mixture into the prepared pan, then top with an even layer of pecans (lay them flat). Set aside.

3. Make the filling: Combine all the ingredients in a small bowl and set aside.

4. Make the dough: Combine all of the ingredients and knead by hand (mix first in a large bowl, then turn out and knead) or in a stand mixer fitted with the dough hook until the dough is elastic.

5. Cover the bowl with plastic wrap and let the dough rise until it has doubled in size, about 1 hour in a warm room.

6. Flour your work surface lightly and turn out the dough. Shape it into a rough rectangle then roll it out to about 12 x 16 inches.

7. Sprinkle the filling on the dough, leaving about 1 inch uncovered on one of the long sides. Starting at the long side with the filling sprinkled to the edge, roll the dough jellyroll style, leaving it a bit loose. When you reach the far end, pinch the seam closed. Cut the dough into 12 equal pieces and place them, cut side down, in the pan with the topping. Flipping the pieces onto a spatula makes moving them from work surface to pan easier.

continued

Nonstick baking spray

FOR THE TOPPING

4 tablespoons unsalted butter

1 cup brown sugar

Pinch kosher salt

1 tablespoon pure vanilla extract

2 tablespoons heavy cream

2 cups pecan halves

FOR THE FILLING

$\frac{1}{2}$ cup plus 1 tablespoon sugar

$\frac{1}{2}$ cup graham cracker crumbs

Pinch kosher salt

FOR THE DOUGH

$\frac{1}{2}$ cup room temperature water

$\frac{1}{2}$ cup heavy cream

1 large egg

$2\frac{1}{4}$ teaspoons active dry yeast

2 tablespoons sugar

1 teaspoon kosher salt

$2\frac{1}{2}$ cups ($11\frac{1}{4}$ ounces) bread flour, plus more as needed

2 tablespoons unsalted butter, at room temperature

8. Gather up any filling that might have fallen out of the rolls and sprinkle it on top of the buns in the pan. Cover the pan with plastic wrap or place it in a large plastic bag and tie the open end closed. Refrigerate overnight or up to 24 hours.

ON BAKING DAY

1. Remove the pan from the refrigerator and heat the oven to 325°F.

2. Remove the plastic from the pan and bake the rolls until golden-brown and the internal temperature is 190°F on an instant-read thermometer, about 45 minutes. Place a large serving plate (or a quarter-sheet baking pan, if you don't have an appropriate plate) on top of the pan and flip the pan and plate over to remove the buns from the pan. Scrape up any topping or nuts left in the pan and place on top of the buns. Serve warm or let cool, as desired.

MAPLE SUGAR FANS

Maple sugar is pretty amazing stuff because it's dried maple syrup. It's also expensive. These buns use maple sugar for the filling and maple syrup in the dough for a double-dose of flavor. If you don't have maple sugar and have a craving for these buns, use white or brown sugar for the filling. It won't be quite the same, but the buns will still be good.

The coffee adds an extra dimension of flavor, but it's not prominent. If you're not fond of coffee or don't want to buy a jar just for this recipe, you can omit it, but I suggest you give it a try first.

MAKES 9 BUNS

ON PREP DAY

1. Spray a 9-inch square baking pan with baking spray.

2. Combine all the dough ingredients in a stand mixer and knead with the dough hook until smooth. You can also mix the ingredients in a large bowl, using a handheld electric mixer, then knead by hand.

3. Cover the bowl with plastic wrap and set aside to rise until the dough has doubled in size, about 1 hour.

4. Flour your work surface and turn out the dough. Roll out the dough to a 12-inch square. Cut the dough into two 6 x 12-inch strips.

5. Brush the surface of each strip with melted butter, then sprinkle with maple sugar. Place one strip on top of the other, sugar side up. Fold the dough in half horizontally, so you now have a strip of dough that's about 3 x 12 inches long. Using a sharp knife, cut the strip into 9 even pieces that are about 1¼ x 3 inches.

6. One at a time, stand the pieces on their folded edge in the prepared pan. You can squish them down a bit if it helps to keep them standing upright. You can place the dough in the pan so all layers are facing the same direction, or alternate the directions for a different look.

7. When all 9 pieces are in the pan, make sure they're about the same height (squish down the ones that are a bit too high), then cover the pan with plastic wrap. Refrigerate overnight or up to 24 hours.

ON BAKING DAY

1. Take the pan out of the refrigerator and heat the oven to 325°F.

2. Remove the plastic and bake the buns until nicely browned and the internal temperature is 190°F on an instant-read thermometer, about 20 minutes. Transfer the buns to a rack to cool.

Nonstick baking spray

FOR THE DOUGH

1 cup room temperature water

2¼ teaspoons active dry yeast

2 tablespoons maple syrup (preferably grade B)

1 tablespoon pure vanilla extract

2½ cups (11¼ ounces) bread flour, plus more as needed

½ teaspoon espresso powder or instant coffee

1½ teaspoons kosher salt

2 tablespoons unsalted butter

FOR THE FILLING

2 tablespoons unsalted butter, melted

2 tablespoons maple sugar

TIP

Maple goes well with nuts, particularly pecans or walnuts. If you like, chop ¼ cup of nuts and sprinkle them on with the maple sugar

Like any sweet roll, if you want these even sweeter, you can drizzle them with confectioners' sugar icing. If you want to infuse it with maple flavor, start with 2 cups of confectioners' sugar and add maple syrup, a teaspoon at a time, until you have a thick but pourable icing. Drizzle it onto the buns when they're still warm, but not hot.

FLATBREADS

SOURDOUGH FLATBREADS

These thick flatbreads are perfect for ripping apart and sopping up sauces or dipping into flavored oils. You could also slice them in half and fill them with flavorful meats or roasted vegetables to make sandwiches, or toast them and spread with butter and a little jam for breakfast.

MAKES EIGHT 4-INCH DIAMETER FLATBREADS

ON PREP DAY 1

Combine the ingredients for the prep day 1 mixture in a medium bowl, stir, and cover. Let sit, covered, at room temperature overnight.

ON PREP DAY 2

1. In the bowl containing the prep day 1 mixture, add the bread flour, 1 tablespoon olive oil, and the salt. Stir to combine, then flour your work surface lightly and turn out the dough. Knead the dough until smooth, soft, and not super-sticky, adding flour only as needed—you want the dough to stay soft.

2. Put the remaining 1 tablespoon of olive oil in a gallon size zip-top plastic bag and put the dough in the bag, massaging the dough to ensure it's coated with oil. Refrigerate overnight or up to 24 hours.

ON BAKING DAY

1. Heat the oven to 350°F and line a baking sheet with parchment paper.

2. Flour your work surface lightly and turn out the dough. Divide the dough into 8 equal pieces, form each into a ball, and then flatten to form a disk. Use a rolling pin and roll each to a disk about 4 inches in diameter.

3. Place the disks on the prepared baking sheet and bake until the flatbreads are lightly browned, about 18 minutes. Transfer to a rack to cool.

FOR PREP DAY 1 MIXTURE

4 ounces (by weight) sourdough starter (see p. 9)

1 cup (4½ ounces) bread flour, plus more as needed

½ cup room temperature water

FOR PREP DAY 2 ADDITIONS

½ cup (2¼ ounces) bread flour

2 tablespoons olive oil, divided

1 teaspoon kosher salt

TIP

Measuring sourdough starter by volume is tricky because of the bubbles. If you don't have a scale to weigh the starter, stir it well to knock down the bubbles as much as possible, then measure out ½ cup of starter.

SEMOLINA FOCACCIA

This focaccia has a rich flavor with a little chew, and it's the perfect vessel for adding herbs and spices, small bits of sun-dried tomato, or a few grates of Parmesan.

But it's also wonderful plain. Try it that way first and serve herbed oil for dipping alongside the bread.

MAKES ONE 9 X 13-INCH LOAF

ON PREP DAY

1. Combine all of the ingredients, reserving 1 tablespoon of the olive oil, in a stand mixer fitted with the paddle attachment or in a large bowl. Knead with the paddle or mix with a wooden spoon or Danish dough whisk until the dough gathers into a ball. This is a very wet and sloppy dough.

2. Drizzle the remaining tablespoon of olive oil into a rimmed quarter-sheet baking pan. Turn out the dough into the middle of the pan. Stretch the dough to fit, dipping your fingers into the oil to keep the dough from sticking to them and to oil the top of the dough.

3. Cover the dough with plastic wrap or put the whole pan in a large plastic bag and tie the open end closed. Refrigerate overnight or up to 24 hours.

ON BAKING DAY

1. Remove the pan from the refrigerator and heat the oven to 375°F.

2. Use your fingers to dimple the top of the loaf: Use your index and middle finger of the same hand and press them into the dough in random spots. Leave the dough plain or sprinkle it with dried herbs or grated Parmesan.

3. Bake at 375°F for 30 minutes or until lightly browned. Let the focaccia cool for a few minutes, then slide it out of the pan and onto a rack to cool.

1¼ cups room temperature water

1 teaspoon active dry yeast

1 cup (6 ounces) semolina

2 cups (9 ounces) bread flour

1 teaspoon kosher salt

1 tablespoon sugar

2 tablespoons olive oil, divided

FLATBREADS *on the* GRILL

Flatbreads are necessary ingredients for a lot of grilled foods—grilled vegetable sandwiches, steak fajitas, or sausage wraps. So why not cook the flatbreads on the grill too? The flatbreads get nicely charred grill marks, they cook quickly, and you won't heat up the house by baking indoors.

If the weather isn't cooperative or if you want to make these in winter when the grill is under a foot of snow, you can heat up a grill pan on the stove.

MAKES SIX 6-INCH FLATBREADS

ON PREP DAY

1. Combine the yeast, sugar, flour, water, and salt in a stand mixer. Using the dough hook, knead the dough until it comes together and looks smooth.

2. Drizzle the olive oil into a gallon-size zip-top plastic bag. Remove the dough from the mixer bowl, form into a ball, and place it in the bag. Remove as much air as possible from the bag, seal it, and refrigerate overnight or up to 2 days.

ON BAKING DAY

1. Remove the dough from the refrigerator, massage it in the bag to knock out some of the air, and let it come to room temperature.

2. Heat a gas or charcoal grill or a grill pan on your stove.

3. Flour your work surface and turn out the dough. Divide it into 6 equal portions and form each portion into a ball. Roll each ball into a thin disk, about 6 inches in diameter and the thickness of a tortilla, adding more flour as needed to keep the dough from sticking.

4. Cook each disk on the hot grill directly on the grates—it should take just a minute or two—until grill marks and some browned parts appear. Flip and cook on the other side for 1 to 2 minutes until the dough is cooked through. Stack grilled flatbreads on top of each other and cover with a clean kitchen towel. Serve warm or at room temperature.

1 teaspoon active dry yeast

1 teaspoon sugar

2½ cups (11¼ ounces) bread flour, plus more as needed

1 cup lukewarm water

1 teaspoon kosher salt

1 tablespoon olive oil

TIP

It can take some practice before you get comfortable putting the flatbreads on the grill. Smaller dough rounds are easier to handle than larger ones, so if you like, divide the dough into more pieces and make smaller flatbreads the first few times you make them.

FRYING PAN FLATBREADS

There are flatbreads that have their roots in a number of cultures, from tortillas to naan to pitas and pizzas. These flatbreads have absolutely no roots in any place except my own kitchen. They're an all-purpose flatbread with a multitude of uses.

MAKES TWELVE 6-INCH FLATBREADS

Cornmeal, for the pan (optional)

1 cup cool water

1 tablespoon apple-cider vinegar

2 1/4 teaspoons active dry yeast

3 cups (13 1/2 ounces) bread flour, plus more as needed

1/4 cup instant mashed potato flakes

1 1/2 teaspoons kosher salt

1 tablespoons sugar

1 tablespoon olive oil

ON PREP DAY

1. Line a baking sheet with parchment paper or sprinkle with cornmeal.

2. Combine the rest of the ingredients in a stand mixer and knead with the dough hook until smooth. You can also mix the ingredients in a large bowl, then knead by hand.

3. Place the dough in a gallon-size zip-top plastic bag and refrigerate overnight or up to 2 days.

ON BAKING DAY

1. Remove the bag from the refrigerator, flour your work surface, and turn out the dough. Divide it into 12 equal pieces and shape each piece into a ball.

2. Heat a cast-iron skillet or a griddle over medium heat until hot but not smoking. I like to use a comal pan because it has low sides, but a regular cast-iron pan, stovetop griddle, or even electric frying pan or griddle will also work.

3. Roll a ball into a flat, round circle about 6 inches in diameter and thinner than a corn tortilla. It will seem ridiculously thin, but it will puff up a lot as it cooks. Roll out more balls as your space allows.

4. Cook each flatbread one at a time in a frying pan, or you can cook several at a time on a griddle. Let the first side brown a little before flipping the flatbread over. These cook through quickly —just a minute or so on the first side and another 30 seconds on the second side. As the flatbreads finish cooking, stack them and cover with a clean kitchen towel. Serve warm or at room temperature.

TIP

Flatbreads are typically cooked just until done, so they're soft and floppy. If you want a crisper flatbread, flip it back onto the first side after the second side is done and continue cooking until that side is crisp and firm, another minute or two.

GLUTEN-FREE FLATBREAD

For help with this gluten-free recipe, I turned to Jeanne Sauvage, author of the book *Gluten-Free Baking for the Holidays*.

These flatbreads can be made smaller or larger, depending on how you'll be using them. Thinner flatbreads make good personal pizza crusts. If you make them thicker, you can slice them in half horizontally, and toast them, like English muffins.

A silicone baking mat is your best friend for making these flatbreads, and once you own one, you'll find plenty of uses for it.

MAKES 4 FLATBREADS, 4 TO 6 INCHES IN DIAMETER

ON PREP DAY

1. Line a baking sheet with a silicone baking mat.

2. Combine all the ingredients in a stand mixer fitted with the paddle attachment. You can also mix the ingredients in a large bowl using a hand-held electric mixer. Beat for 5 minutes. The texture won't be like bread dough; instead, it will seem a little gluey—like mashed potatoes that have gone wrong.

3. Divide the dough into 4 pieces, transfer to the baking sheet, and then use your fingers to form each into a rough flat round 4 to 6 inches in diameter. Cover the pan with plastic wrap and refrigerate overnight or up to 24 hours.

ON BAKING DAY

1. Remove the pan from the refrigerator, and heat the oven to 375°F.

2. Remove the plastic from the pan. Bake the flatbreads until they are browned on the bottom and a few brown spots appear on the top, about 25 minutes. The internal temperature of the flatbreads should be 205°F on an instant-read thermometer. Remove the pan from the oven and transfer the flatbreads to a rack to cool. If you want to serve these warm, heat in the oven or toast in a hot cast-iron pan or on a griddle.

- $1\frac{1}{2}$ cups ($8\frac{1}{4}$ ounces) King Arthur Flour gluten-free multipurpose flour mix
- 1 teaspoon kosher salt
- 1 teaspoon xanthan gum
- 1 tablespoon sugar
- $\frac{3}{4}$ cup room temperature water
- 1 tablespoon olive oil
- 1 teaspoon white vinegar

TIP

For a little extra flavor, brush these flatbreads with butter or oil or sprinkle with a bit of cheese (hard like Parmesan or any melting cheese) about a minute before they're done baking. Depending on how you're using the flatbreads, you can also sprinkle them with sesame seeds, finely chopped nuts, black pepper, or coarse salt before baking.

NAAN

One of the most recognizable things about naan bread is its unique shape. Some people describe it as a teardrop; some call it a snowshoe. But for me, I'd have to say that it's a comic exclamation point without the dot.

MAKES FOUR 4 X 8-INCH FLATBREADS

ON PREP DAY

1. Combine all the ingredients except the oil and the butter in a stand mixer and knead with the dough hook until smooth. You can also mix the ingredients in a large bowl, then knead by hand.

2. Drizzle the olive oil into a gallon-size zip-top plastic bag and place the dough in the bag. Refrigerate overnight or up to 2 days.

ON BAKING DAY

1. Heat the oven to 400°F and place a baking sheet in the oven.

2. Flour your work surface and turn out the dough. Divide it into 4 equal pieces and shape each piece into a ball.

3. Flatten the pieces and shape them into a teardrop shape. You can stretch and press them by hand or use a rolling pin. You're looking for a shape that's about 4 inches wide at the widest part and about 8 inches long.

4. Remove the baking sheet from the oven and carefully place the dough on the sheet. Be careful   the pan will be quite hot. Return the pan to the oven and bake the naan until they're browned on the bottom, puffy, and have a few brown spots on top, about 12 minutes. Transfer the naan to a rack and brush with melted butter. Serve warm or at room temperature.

1/2 cup Greek-style plain yogurt
3/4 cup room temperature water
2 1/4 teaspoons active dry yeast
1 tablespoon sugar
3 cups (13 1/2 ounces) bread flour, plus more as needed
1 1/2 teaspoons kosher salt
1 tablespoon olive oil
1 tablespoon salted butter, melted

TIP

Although it's not traditional, these naan are quite tasty topped with sesame or nigella seeds. Even less traditional, brush them with flavored butter rather than plain.

RYE SANDWICH WRAPS
with CARAWAY

These wraps are like pita bread, but with rye and caraway seed. I like them stuffed with chunked chicken, shredded lettuce, and a creamy dressing. They're also great served as a simple bread, torn apart for eating, or ripped into pieces and baked for crackers.

The rye flour makes these breads a little less stretchy, which means they're prone to cracking if you fold them too tightly. The added gluten helps with that, as does gentle warming before folding.

MAKES 8 WRAPS, 6 TO 8 INCHES IN DIAMETER

ON PREP DAY

1. Combine all of the ingredients, reserving 1 tablespoon of oil, and knead by hand (mix first in a large bowl, then turn out and knead) or in a stand mixer fitted with the dough hook, until the dough is elastic.

2. Drizzle the remaining 1 tablespoon of oil into a gallon-size zip-top plastic bag, then add the dough. Squish and massage the dough a bit to coat it with oil. Zip the top of the bag and refrigerate overnight or up to 24 hours.

ON BAKING DAY

1. Remove the dough from the refrigerator and heat the oven to 350°F.

2. Line four baking sheets with parchment paper.

3. Flour your work surface lightly, turn out the dough, then divide the dough into 8 equal pieces. Form each piece into a ball, then flatten each ball with the palm of your hand.

4. Working with one piece of dough at a time, use a rolling pin to roll each one into a flat disk that's 6 to 8 inches in diameter. Place 2 disks on each prepared baking sheet and bake at 350°F for about 6 minutes, until the breads are puffy and have some light browning on the edges and some brown spots on the underside. If you're baking several sheets at once, rotate their oven positions about halfway through baking. Remove the flatbreads from the baking sheet and cool on a rack.

$1\frac{1}{4}$ cups room temperature water

$\frac{1}{4}$ cup instant mashed potato flakes

1 teaspoon active dry yeast

1 cup ($4\frac{1}{2}$ ounces) rye flour

$1\frac{1}{2}$ cups ($6\frac{3}{4}$ ounces) bread flour, plus more as needed

1 tablespoon vital wheat gluten

1 tablespoon sugar

1 teaspoon kosher salt

1 tablespoon caraway seed

2 tablespoons olive oil, divided

TIP

If you want to serve the flatbreads warm, stick them in a 200°F oven for about 10 minutes, in the microwave wrapped in a clean kitchen towel for 10 seconds, or in a dry cast-iron skillet for 30 seconds on each side.

WHOLE WHEAT PITA BREAD

These whole wheat flatbreads are perfect for ripping, dipping, or topping. I like them topped with greens dressed with balsamic vinegar and good olive oil and a crumble of feta cheese.

These are best served the day they're made, but the good news is that you don't have to make them all on the same day. The dough is good for at least 2 days and up to 4.

MAKES SIX 6-INCH FLATBREADS OR TWELVE 5-INCH FLATBREADS

ON PREP DAY

1. Combine all the ingredients in a stand mixer with a dough hook and knead until a ball forms.

2. There's probably residual oil in the spoon you used to measure the oil. Drizzle that into a gallon-size zip-top plastic bag, or just add a teaspoon of oil to the bag. Place the dough in the bag, close the top, and refrigerate overnight or up to 4 days.

ON BAKING DAY

1. Heat the oven to 375°F and line several baking sheets with parchment paper.

2. Flour your work surface lightly. Turn out the dough and divide it into 6 pieces (for 6-inch diameter pitas) or 12 pieces (for 5-inch diameter pitas).

3. Form the pieces into balls, flatten them into disks, then use a rolling pin to roll them to the desired size. Place some on a prepared baking sheet; you can place the disks close together, but make sure they aren't overlapping.

4. Bake until the bottoms have a few brown spots and the tops look dry and are lighter in color, about 5 minutes. It's fine if the breads bubble or puff up like balloons in the oven—they will deflate as they cool.

5. Continue rolling and baking the pitas until all the dough is used up. As the pitas get done, stack them on top of each other, and cover with a clean kitchen towel. Serve warm or at room temperature.

1 cup room temperature water

2¼ teaspoons active dry yeast

1½ cups (6¾ ounces) whole wheat flour

1½ cups (6¾ ounces) bread flour, plus more as needed

1 teaspoon kosher salt

2 tablespoons olive oil, plus another 1 teaspoon as needed for the bag

TIP

Leftover pita bread makes great crackers. Cut it into wedges and bake at 250°F until they're completely crisp.

FLOUR TORTILLAS

Making your own flour tortillas is pretty easy. But even the best tortillas are rather bland. The overnight rest not only improves the flavor of these tortillas but also means you can have fresh, hot tortillas in a lot less time.

Stack cooked tortillas and wrap in a clean kitchen towel to keep warm for a short time, or place that bundle in a warm (200°F) oven for a little longer.

MAKES 8 TORTILLAS, 7 TO 8 INCHES IN DIAMETER

ON PREP DAY

1. Combine all the ingredients in a stand mixer and knead with a dough hook until a ball of dough forms. You can also mix the ingredients in a large bowl and knead by hand.

2. Place the dough in a gallon-size zip-top plastic bag and refrigerate overnight or up to 2 days.

ON BAKING DAY

1. Flour your work surface and turn out the dough. It might stick a bit to the bag, so use a dough scraper if needed.

2. Heat a large cast-iron skillet or a griddle on the stove over medium heat.

3. Divide the dough into 8 pieces, shape each into a ball, and then flatten into a disk. Using a rolling pin, roll the disks into 7- or 8-inch diameter rounds, depending on whether you prefer smaller, thicker home-style tortillas or larger thinner ones. At 8 inches, the dough will seem impossibly thin, but it will puff quite a bit as it cooks.

4. As the tortillas are formed, place them in the skillet or on the griddle. Cook each tortilla until brown spots appear on the bottom, then flip it over and cook for another 30 seconds or so. You'll see bubbles rising on the surface of the tortillas as they cook, and they might puff like balloons. That's normal. Each tortilla should take only about 3 minutes total, depending on the heat of the skillet or griddle. Feel free to cook several tortillas at the same time if your cooking surface is large enough. As the tortillas are cooked, stack them on top of each other and cover with a clean kitchen towel. Serve warm or at room temperature.

- ¾ cup room temperature water
- 1 teaspoon instant yeast
- 1 teaspoon sugar
- 2 cups (9 ounces) bread flour, plus more as needed
- 1 teaspoon kosher salt

TIP

There's no reason you can't season your tortillas to pair with your food. Herbs like oregano, garlic powder, or a pinch of chili powder can liven them up. A little goes a long way, though, so start with ½ teaspoon of your flavoring or spice and add more the next time if it's not quite enough.

CIABATTA

Ciabatta is a slipperlike bread, meaning it's sort of flat and a long oval shape. It's normally made from very wet dough, which is one reason why it tends to spread sideways rather than rise upward.

If you haven't worked with wet doughs, there are a few things you should know. First, don't add more flour than what's called for. There's a tendency to want to add more flour to make it less sticky, but that will make the dough more firm and more apt to rise high instead of spread.

Wet doughs also tend to result in uneven hole structure, which is what's expected in this type of bread. You should see smaller holes, larger holes, and medium holes.

This bread takes several days to make, but none of the steps are difficult or time-consuming.

MAKES ONE 14-INCH LOAF

1¼ cups room temperature water

1 teaspoon active dry yeast

1 tablespoon sugar

2¾ cups (12⅜ ounces) bread flour, plus more as needed

1 teaspoon kosher salt

1 tablespoon olive oil, for the bag

Cornmeal, for the pan

Rice flour, for sprinkling on the dough (optional)

ON PREP DAY 1

1. Combine the first five ingredients in a gallon-size zip-top plastic bag. Squeeze and massage the bag until the ingredients are combined. The dough should become wet and sticky—not as wet as a batter, but easy to mash together.

2. Add the oil and continue massaging the dough. You're not trying to work the oil into the dough but simply coating the dough so that it doesn't stick to the bag. Close the top of the bag and refrigerate overnight or up to 24 hours.

ON PREP DAY 2

1. Line a baking sheet with parchment paper, then sprinkle it with cornmeal.

2. Remove the dough from the refrigerator and squish it around in the bag to get oil between the bag and the dough so it releases easily. Flour your work surface generously and turn out the dough into a roughly formed square.

3. Fold the far side of the dough toward you over the bottom half of dough, leaving about 1 inch uncovered. Press down to seal. Now fold the dough from right to left, bottom to top, and left to right in the same way. When you're done, the dough should feel much firmer, but still very soft.

continued

4. Let the dough rest for 10 to 20 minutes, then fold from the top and bottom only (going all the way to the edge), forming a long loaf about 12 inches long, and seal the seam. The dough will decide for itself how wide it will be, since it's still soft and floppy. Place the dough, seam side down, on the prepared baking sheet. Use your hands to shape it into a somewhat even loaf with rounded ends.

5. Sprinkle rice flour (or bread flour) on the dough to keep it from sticking to the plastic wrap. Cover the pan with plastic and refrigerate overnight or up to 24 hours.

ON BAKING DAY

1. Remove the pan from the refrigerator. Heat the oven to 375°F.

2. Remove the plastic from the pan and bake the bread until it is golden-brown, about 40 minutes. Transfer the loaf on the parchment to a rack and cool completely before slicing.

BASIC PIZZA DOUGH

This basic pizza dough is a simple blank canvas for the toppings of your choice. Roll it super thin, if you like, or leave it a little thicker. Divide it into smaller pizzas, or even minis. With a ball of dough in your refrigerator, home-baked pizza can be a fast weeknight meal.

MAKES TWO 10-INCH PIZZAS

ON PREP DAY

Mix the first four ingredients in a gallon-size zip-top plastic bag. You don't need to knead the ingredients; just make sure they are evenly mixed and that there are no dry bits in the dough. Zip the top of the bag and refrigerate overnight or up 2 days.

ON BAKING DAY

1. Remove the dough from the refrigerator and heat the oven to 550°F. If you are using a baking stone, heat that in the oven. If you don't have a baking stone, the pizzas can be baked on a baking sheet sprinkled with cornmeal. Because you're heating the oven to a high temperature and want the stone thoroughly heated, it's best to let the oven heat for at least 45 minutes.

2. Flour your work surface and turn out the dough. Divide it into 2 equal pieces. If you're only making one pizza, wrap and refrigerate the other piece for up to 2 days. Or bake it without toppings and finish later.

3. Roll 1 piece of dough into a circle between 8 and 12 inches in diameter, depending on how thick you like your pizza.

4. Sprinkle a pizza peel with cornmeal. If you don't have a peel, sprinkle the back side of a baking sheet with cornmeal. Whether you are using a peel or baking sheet, grab one edge of the dough round and pull it onto the surface; reshape the dough as necessary.

5. Working quickly, top the pizza as desired, slide it onto the baking stone (or leave it on the baking sheet), and bake for 8 minutes, or until the edges of the pizza are browned and the cheese is melted.

3 cups (13$\frac{1}{2}$ ounces) unbleached all-purpose flour, plus more as needed

1$\frac{1}{4}$ cup room temperature water

1 teaspoon instant yeast

1$\frac{1}{2}$ teaspoons kosher salt

Cornmeal, for the pizza peel or baking sheet

TIP

If you're not adept at sliding a pizza from a peel onto a baking stone, put the pizza on a piece of parchment paper on the peel, then slide the parchment—with the pizza on it—onto the stone.

GRANDMA PIZZA

This pizza is the mutant stepchild of pizza, focaccia, and pan pizza. I have no idea who originally called it "grandma pizza." It's a pizza style that some moms made when I was a youngster, but the recipes were attributed to grandma.

If you're a fan of cold pizza for breakfast, give this one a try. It's also great reheated gently in the microwave or in a toaster oven.

MAKES ONE 9 X 13-INCH PIZZA

ON PREP DAY

1. Combine the yeast, bread flour, salt, and water in a bowl. Mix until well combined. The dough will be rough and shaggy, but that's just fine.

2. Drizzle the olive oil into a gallon-size zip-top plastic bag. Transfer the dough to the bag, massage the dough so that it's coated with oil, seal the bag, and refrigerate the dough overnight or up to 2 days.

ON BAKING DAY

1. Remove the dough from the refrigerator and heat the oven to 375°F.

2. Transfer the dough, along with all of the oil, to a rimmed quarter-sheet baking pan. Use your fingertips to poke, prod, and encourage the dough to spread to fill the pan. If it doesn't want to fit tightly into the corners, that's fine.

3. Spread the tomatoes over the top of the dough, leaving about $1/2$ inch uncoated around the edges of the pan. Scatter the cheese on top of the tomatoes, then sprinkle with basil, if using. (You can add more toppings, but if you pile them on or if they're wet, you'll need to adjust the baking time.)

4. Bake the pizza until the cheese is bubbly and the dough is nicely browned and firm, about 40 minutes.

FOR THE DOUGH

1 teaspoon instant yeast

3 cups ($13^{1}/_{2}$ ounces) bread flour

1 teaspoon kosher salt

$1^{1}/_{4}$ cups room temperature water

2 tablespoons olive oil

FOR THE TOPPING

$1/_{2}$ cup canned crushed tomatoes

4 ounces mozzarella cheese, sliced or shredded

Sliced fresh basil (optional)

WHOLE WHEAT *and* PARMESAN PIZZA CRUST

Pizza isn't the first thing you think of when someone mentions healthy food, but you can make it better for you by adding whole wheat flour to the dough. Then, for more flavor, there's Parmesan.

   This is a great base for any pizza, whether it's a classic style with tomato sauce, a white pizza, or a vegetarian delight.

MAKES 2 PIZZAS, 8 TO 12 INCHES IN DIAMETER

ON PREP DAY

1. Combine the water, sugar, yeast, and 2 cups of the bread flour in a medium bowl or a stand mixer. Mix well (with a spoon by hand or the dough hook in the mixer), then set aside (uncovered) for 10 minutes.

2. Add the remaining 1 cup of bread flour and the 1 cup of whole wheat flour to the mixture. Mix until combined, then knead in a stand mixer fitted with the dough hook or turn out onto your counter (lightly flour first) and knead by hand until the dough is smooth. Add the salt and Parmesan cheese and continue kneading until they are well distributed through the dough.

3. Drizzle the olive oil into a gallon-size zip-top plastic bag. Transfer the dough to the bag and squish the dough around a bit to coat it with oil. Close the bag and refrigerate the dough overnight or up to 2 days.

ON BAKING DAY

1. Remove the dough from the refrigerator and heat the oven to 550°F. If you are using a baking stone, heat that in the oven. If you don't have a baking stone, the pizza can be baked on a baking sheet sprinkled with cornmeal. Because you're heating the oven to a high temperature and want the stone thoroughly heated, it's best to let the oven heat for at least 45 minutes.

2. Flour your work surface and turn out the dough. Divide it into 2 equal pieces. If you're only making one pizza, wrap and refrigerate the other piece for up to 2 days. Or bake it without toppings and finish later.

3. Roll 1 piece of dough into a circle between 8 and 12 inches in diameter, depending on how thick you like your pizza.

4. Sprinkle a pizza peel with cornmeal. If you don't have a peel, sprinkle the back side of a baking sheet with cornmeal. Whether using a peel or baking sheet, grab one edge of the dough round and pull it onto the surface; reshape the dough as necessary. You can also roll out the dough on parchment, then transfer the parchment with dough to the peel and stone.

5. Working quickly, top the pizza as desired, slide it onto the baking stone (or leave it on the baking sheet), and bake for 8 minutes, until the edges of the pizza are browned and the cheese is melted.

1 1/2 cups lukewarm water

1 tablespoon sugar

1 teaspoon instant yeast

3 cups (13 1/2 ounces) bread flour, divided, plus more as needed

1 cup whole wheat flour

1 teaspoon kosher salt

2 ounces grated Parmesan cheese

1 tablespoon olive oil

Cornmeal, for the pizza peel or baking sheet

PIZZA *on the* GRILL

The great thing about cooking pizza on the grill is that you won't heat up the house. The tricky thing is getting the top of the pizza cooked well enough before the bottom burns. It might take a few tries before you figure out exactly how to set up the grill for the best heating, but once you know that formula, you'll turn out perfect pizzas every time.

MAKES TWO 12-INCH PIZZAS

ON PREP DAY

1. Combine the yeast, water, sugar, and semolina flour in a stand mixer or in a medium bowl if you'll be hand kneading. Stir to combine and let the mixture rest for 5 to 10 minutes. Add the bread flour and salt and knead with the dough hook if you're using a stand mixer (or turn it out onto your counter and knead by hand) until the dough is smooth.

2. Drizzle the oil in a gallon-size zip-top plastic bag and transfer the dough to the bag. Massage the dough so that it's coated on all sides with the oil, then seal the bag and refrigerate overnight or up to 2 days.

ON BAKING DAY

1. When you're ready to grill the pizza, remove the dough from the refrigerator and let it warm up on your counter while the grill heats.

2. Heat the grill (gas or charcoal) on high for 20 minutes. If you'll be using a pizza stone or cast-iron griddle pan, put that on the grill grates while the grill heats. (Some pizza stones are not safe for grilling, so check yours to be sure.) Set up the grill so there is direct heat around the pizza stone or pan and indirect heat directly below it. If you will be putting the dough directly on the grill grates, wipe the grates with a bit of olive oil and be sure the heat is set to indirect.

3. Divide the dough in half and put one half back in the bag and refrigerate for up to 2 days if you aren't going to make a second pizza. Lightly flour your work surface, and roll out the dough into a circle about 12 inches in diameter (or whatever shape will fit your baking stone or grill). You can also use your hands to gently stretch the dough into shape. Sprinkle a pizza peel (or whatever you'll use to transport the dough to the grill) with cornmeal. Transfer the dough to the peel and add your toppings. Move quickly when you're adding toppings, then give the peel a few gentle shakes to make sure the dough isn't sticking.

2 ¼ teaspoons instant yeast

1 cup lukewarm water

1 teaspoon sugar

½ cup (3 ounces) semolina flour

2 cups (9 ounces) bread flour, plus more as needed

1 teaspoon kosher salt

1 tablespoon olive oil

Cornmeal, for the pizza peel

4. Transfer the pizza to the hot stone, or directly on the grates, close the lid quickly, and let the pizza cook for 8 minutes. Open the lid just enough to peek inside to check the pizza. You don't want to open the lid all the way because you'll lose all the overhead heat. Cook for a few minutes more, if needed, to melt the cheese.

5. If the bottom of the pizza is getting overdone and the top is still underdone, turn on your oven's broiler and slide the pizza underneath for 30 seconds to finish it. Slice the pizza and serve.

TIP

A drizzle of olive oil on top of the dough will help keep wet ingredients from getting the dough soggy, but the toppings are up to you. A thin layer of canned crushed tomatoes and a few slices of cheese is plenty if your dough is flavorful. Add most fresh herbs, like basil, to the pizza after it comes off the grill for the most flavor.

Any toppings other than marinara sauce or tomatoes and cheese should be cooked and warm before they're added to the pizza because they won't be on the grill long enough to cook.

SWEET BREAKFAST ROUNDS
with DRIED BLUEBERRIES

These sweet breads are fatter than a pancake but thinner than a bagel. They're great sliced horizontally and slathered with butter or cream cheese, but they're just as good eaten plain, next to a plate of bacon and eggs. They're good toasted, too. Or slice and spread with peanut butter.

These rounds freeze well. Slice them first, then wrap them well and stash in the freezer. When you want one for breakfast, pop the halves in the toaster to defrost and toast at the same time.

MAKES 8 ROUNDS

ON PREP DAY

1. Combine all of the ingredients and knead by hand (mix first in a medium bowl, then turn out and knead) or in a stand mixer fitted with the dough hook, until the dough is elastic.

2. Cover the bowl with plastic wrap and let the dough rise until it has doubled in size, about 1 hour in a warm room.

3. Line a baking sheet with parchment paper. Flour your work surface, turn out the dough, and divide it into 8 pieces. Form the pieces into balls, then flatten them into disks that are about $3\frac{1}{2}$ to 4 inches in diameter; you can do this by pressing and stretching the dough with your fingers. Cover the pan with plastic wrap and refrigerate overnight or up to 24 hours.

ON BAKING DAY

1. Remove the pan from the refrigerator and heat the oven to 350°F.

2. Remove the plastic from the pan, then bake the buns until they are golden-brown, about 35 minutes. Transfer the buns to a rack and let cool.

1 cup room temperature water

$2\frac{1}{4}$ teaspoons active dry yeast

$\frac{1}{4}$ cup sugar

$\frac{1}{4}$ cup instant mashed potato flakes

$2\frac{1}{2}$ cups ($11\frac{1}{4}$ ounces) bread flour, plus more as needed

1 teaspoon kosher salt

3 tablespoons unsalted butter

$\frac{1}{4}$ cup dried blueberries

CHICAGO-STYLE PAN PIZZA

Love it or hate it, deep-dish pizza is popular in Chicago, its city of birth. But like thin-crust pizza, styles vary from one place to another. This pizza is on the thinner side, so you can pick up a pie-shaped wedge and eat it out of hand. But feel free to go after it with a knife and fork, if you prefer.

The cheese here is important. Choose a low-moisture mozzarella that's sold in a ball rather than a brick. While fresh mozzarella is wonderful, it would give off too much moisture during cooking.

I don't buy too many seasoning mixes, but there are a few I like, and pizza seasoning is one. I use it for pizza but also sometimes on bread, croutons, and chicken. Italian seasoning would also be fine, or just use a mixture of 1 teaspoon oregano and ½ teaspoon basil.

MAKES TWO 9-INCH PIZZAS

1¼ cups room temperature water

2¼ teaspoons active dry yeast

1 teaspoon sugar

2½ cups (11¼ ounces) bread flour

½ cup (3 ounces) semolina flour

1½ teaspoons kosher salt

3 tablespoons olive oil, divided

Cornmeal, for the pan

1½ pounds low-moisture mozzarella cheese

1 pound bulk Italian sausage

2 cups canned crushed tomatoes

2 teaspoons pizza seasoning (store-bought or homemade)

ON PREP DAY

1. Combine the water, yeast, sugar, flours, salt, and 2 tablespoons olive oil in a stand mixer fitted with the dough hook and knead until the dough comes together in a ball. You can also mix the ingredients in a large bowl and knead by hand.

2. Drizzle the remaining 1 tablespoon olive oil into a gallon-size zip-top plastic bag, then add the dough and close the bag. Let it rest at room temperature for 1 hour—it will expand during that time. Squish and massage the dough in the bag to knock out the air, open the bag to release the air and then close the bag again. Refrigerate overnight or up to 2 days.

ON BAKING DAY

1. Heat the oven to 325°F.

2. Sprinkle cornmeal on the bottom of a 9-inch springform pan. You can also use a 9-inch cake pan but it's easier to remove the pizza from the springform.

3. Remove the dough from the bag and divide it into 2 equal pieces. Form 1 piece into a round disk, then place it in the pan and press and stretch it to fit all the way to the edges, making sure it's touching the sides of the pan all the way around.

4. Cut the mozzarella into ⅛-inch slices and arrange half of the slices on top of the dough. Arrange half of the sausage on top of the cheese. (The sausage goes on raw; press it onto the dough evenly or scatter lumpy pieces around evenly.) Mix the crushed tomatoes with the pizza seasoning and spread half of the sauce on top of the meat.

5. Use the second piece of dough and the remaining ingredients to make a second pizza in the same way.

6. Instead of baking right away, let the pizza rest for up to an hour. If you let it rest, the crust will be more airy, but if you bake the pizza immediately, it will still rise. Bake the pizza until the cheese is melted, bubbly, and browned in spots, and the crust is browned, about 1 hour. Use an instant-read thermometer to check the meat, which should register at least 165°F; the crust should register 195°F.

7. Release the springform clasp, remove the ring, and transfer the pizza to a cutting board for slicing. Removing the pizza from a cake pan is a little more difficult. Use two small flexible spatulas to get under the pizza on two sides and lift it out of the pan, or cut it directly in the pan, but be careful you don't damage the pan. Serve hot.

TIP

If you want to add extra toppings like peppers, onions, or mushrooms, cook them first to remove the moisture that would escape during cooking. You don't want a soggy pizza. Low-moisture toppings like pepperoni can go on as is.

PASTRIES

CHERRY TURNOVERS

Some folks might say I'm a bit fanatical about making things completely from scratch. I mean, I bake all of our bread. But even I have my limits. Cherry pie filling, for example. It's not the filling-making that thwarts me; it's the cherry pitting. I've done it and I may do it again, but I prefer not to.

Sometimes I can buy frozen pitted pie cherries at the farmer's market, but there are also a number of good prepared pie fillings available these days. I'm perfectly willing to buy a good pie filling, which has the advantage of being available all year long, so I can concentrate on the pastry.

If you're a pie filling expert, you can, of course, use your own cherry pie filling for this recipe.

MAKES 18 TURNOVERS

ON PREP DAY 1

1. Put the yeast, milk, egg, sugar, and extracts in a medium bowl. Whisk to combine.

2. Put the flour, almond meal, and salt in a food processor and pulse a few times to distribute the salt. Cut the butter into a few pieces and add to the food processor. Pulse until the butter pieces are no larger than a lima bean. It's fine if some pieces (or most of them) are smaller.

3. Transfer the flour-butter mixture to the bowl with the liquid. Stir gently until combined. The mixture should be wet, so don't worry if it seems loose. If it's not a wet mixture or if you see dry spots in the flour, drizzle in more milk, 1 tablespoon at a time, to moisten the dough. Cover the bowl and refrigerate overnight.

ON PREP DAY 2

1. Flour your work surface and turn out the dough. Flour the top of the dough, then pat it into a rough square. Using a rolling pin, roll the dough to about 18 inches square, though the shape doesn't matter so much. The point is to flatten the bits of butter that will make the buttery, flaky layers, but you don't want the butter to soften so much that it starts to mix with the flour, so work as quickly as possible. Flour your work surface and the top of the dough as needed to keep the dough from sticking.

2. Take the left third of the dough and fold it over the middle, then fold the right side over the middle, like you would fold a letter. Use a dough scraper under the

continued

2¼ teaspoons active dry yeast

¾ cup milk, plus more as needed

1 large egg

⅓ cup sugar

1 teaspoon pure vanilla extract

½ teaspoon almond extract

2½ cups (11¼ ounces) bread flour, plus more as needed

½ cup (2 ounces) almond meal

1 teaspoon kosher salt

2 sticks butter, cold (1 salted, 1 unsalted)

One 21-ounce can or jar cherry pie filling

Egg wash (1 large egg beaten with 1 tablespoon water; optional)

Sugar, for sprinkling (optional)

dough to help lift it and fold it over. It's fine if the dough is sloppy and wants to break apart. Now, fold the top third down over the middle, then fold the bottom third up. You should have a fat square of dough.

3. Roll the dough to about 16 inches square, then fold following the same process as above. This time the dough should be easier to roll and fold.

4. Roll out the dough to 16 inches square one more time and fold as before. If at any time during the roll-and-fold process you feel that the butter is getting soft and squishy, put the dough in the refrigerator for 10 minutes or so to firm up the butter—you don't want it to mix with the flour.

5. Flour the dough, wrap it in plastic, and place in a clean zip-top plastic bag. Refrigerate overnight or up to 2 days.

ON BAKING DAY

1. Line a baking sheet with parchment paper. Remove the dough from the refrigerator, divide it in half, and rewrap half and return to the refrigerator.

2. Flour your work surface and roll the dough to 12 inches square. Cut the dough into three 4-inch rows both horizontally and vertically so you end up with 9 even squares (each about 4 x 4 inches).

3. Spoon a generous teaspoon of the pie filling into the center of each square. You should use up about half of the pie filling.

4. Put some water in a small bowl and use your finger or a pastry brush to lightly moisten the edges of the squares. Fold each square into a triangle—you'll need to stretch the dough a bit to cover the filling. Press a fork along the joined edges of the pastry to help seal it. Place the filled pastries on the prepared baking sheet, leaving space between them to rise. Continue making pastries with the second half of the dough and the rest of the pie filling, or leave the dough refrigerated for another day.

5. Cover the pan with plastic wrap and set aside for 20 to 30 minutes. Meanwhile, heat the oven to 400°F. After 20 to 30 minutes, the dough won't seem to have risen, but it should feel puffy rather than firm.

6. Remove the plastic, brush the top of the turnovers with egg wash (if using), and sprinkle with sugar, if desired. Use a sharp knife to cut a few slits in the top of the pastries. Bake the turnovers until they're nicely browned, 15 to 20 minutes. Transfer to a rack to cool before serving.

LEMON DANISH

If you love tart flavors, then this pastry is for you. The bright and sunny lemon curd is more tart than sweet, and it's balanced by the richness of the cheese layer. If you'd prefer something less tart but still lemony, use Meyer lemons or use one-third of the lemon curd for each pastry instead of half.

You can also add a small amount of lemon oil to the dough to make the pastry lemony to match the filling. The oil you want is intended as a flavoring, not the gently flavored lemon olive oil.

I like the salt balance that comes from using 1 stick of salted butter and 1 stick of unsalted, but I'll admit that it's subtle. You can certainly use 2 sticks of salted or unsalted butter, if you prefer.

MAKES TWO 7 X 14-INCH PASTRIES

ON PREP DAY 1

1. Make the lemon curd filling: Whisk the yolks, egg, sugar, lemon juice, butter, and salt in a heavy-bottomed pot. The butter won't incorporate, but that's fine. Heat on medium low and stir until the mixture is thick enough to coat the back of a spoon and hold a line drawn through it with a finger.

2. Remove the pot from the heat and pour the mixture though a fine-mesh strainer, to catch any errant bits of egg, and into a storage container. Cover and refrigerate until needed. It will thicken a bit more as it cools.

3. Make the cheese filling: In a small bowl, whisk together the cream cheese, ricotta, and sugar until smooth. Transfer to a storage container, cover, and refrigerate until needed.

4. Make the pastry: Whisk the egg, water, yeast, and sugar in a medium bowl.

5. Put the flour, salt, and lemon oil (if using) in a food processor and pulse a few times to distribute the salt. Cut the butter into a few pieces and put it in the food processor. Pulse until the butter pieces are no larger than a lima bean. It's fine if some pieces (or most of them) are smaller.

6. Transfer the flour-butter mixture to the bowl with the sugar-water mixture. Stir gently until combined. The mixture should be wet, so don't worry if it seems loose. If it's not a wet mixture or if you see dry spots in the flour, drizzle in more water, 1 tablespoon at a time, to moisten the dough.

7. Cover the bowl with plastic wrap and refrigerate overnight.

FOR THE LEMON CURD FILLING
3 large egg yolks
1 large whole egg
1 cup sugar
1/2 cup fresh lemon juice (about 2 1/2 medium lemons)
1 tablespoon unsalted butter
Pinch of salt

FOR THE CHEESE FILLING
4 ounces cream cheese
2 ounces ricotta cheese
2 tablespoons sugar

FOR THE PASTRY
1 large egg
3/4 cup cool water
2 1/4 teaspoons active dry yeast
1/4 cup sugar
2 1/4 cups (11 1/4 ounces) bread flour, plus more as needed
1 teaspoon kosher salt
1/4 teaspoon lemon oil (optional)
2 sticks butter (1 salted, 1 unsalted)

Egg wash (1 large egg beaten with 1 tablespoon water)
Pearl sugar or granulated sugar, for garnish (optional)

ON PREP DAY 2

1. Flour your work surface and turn out the dough. Flour the top of the dough, then pat it into a rough square. Using a rolling pin, roll the dough to about 18 inches square, though the shape doesn't matter so much. The point is to flatten the bits of butter that will make the buttery, flaky layers, but you don't want the butter to soften so much that it starts to mix with the flour, so work as quickly as possible. Flour your work surface and the top of the dough as needed to keep the dough from sticking.

2. Take the left third of the dough and fold it over the middle, then fold the right side over the middle, like you would fold a letter. Use a dough scraper under the dough to help lift it and fold it over. It's fine if the dough is sloppy and wants to break apart. Now, fold the top third down over the middle, then fold the bottom third up. You should have a fat square of dough.

3. Roll the dough to about 16 inches square, then perform the same folding process as above. This time the dough should be easier to roll and fold.

4. Once you have a fat square of dough, roll it one more time to 16 inches square and fold as before. If at any time during the rolling and folding you feel the butter getting soft and squishy, put the dough in the refrigerator for 10 minutes to firm up the butter—you don't want it to mix with the flour.

5. After the third roll-and-fold process, flour the dough, wrap it in plastic, and place it in a clean zip-top plastic bag. Refrigerate overnight or up to 2 days.

ON PREP DAY 3

1. Remove the dough from the refrigerator, divide it in half, and rewrap half and return to the refrigerator.

2. Flour your work surface and roll the dough to 9 x 16 inches. Transfer it to a piece of parchment paper that will fit a baking sheet.

3. Spread half the cheese mixture lengthwise down the middle third of the dough, leaving about an inch uncovered on the two short ends. Spread half of the lemon curd on top of the cheese, leaving about a ¼-inch border of cheese uncovered all along the edges.

4. Using a sharp knife, pizza cutter, or pastry cutter, cut slits from the edge of the dough to within about ½ inch of the filling along both long sides, leaving about 1 inch between the slits. This creates strips that will be folded over the filled center of the dough.

5. To start the folding process, first fold over the two short ends so they just cover the filling. Then begin folding the strips from the edges over the center of the dough, alternating strips from one side of the pastry and then the other and

continued

continued

TIP

You can make the fillings up to 2 days ahead of time and keep them refrigerated, or make them the day you need them, leaving enough time for the curd to cool completely.

VARIATION

If you're more a fan of lime than lemon, make a lime curd and use it in the filling. Replace the ½ cup fresh lemon juice with ½ cup fresh lime juice. The method for making the curd is the same as for lemon.

Lime curd will be the same golden yellow color as lemon curd. If you prefer it to be green-tinged, add a bit of food coloring.

letting them overlap in the center. The dough will stretch quite easily to allow you to do this. Flatten out any creases as you fold the strips so they lay flat. While you're not actually braiding, you will end up with a braided effect. Slide the parchment, with the pastry on it, onto a baking sheet, then nudge and tuck where needed to straighten the pastry. Cover the pastry with plastic wrap and set aside for 20 minutes.

6. Make a second Danish from the reserved dough, or keep that dough for another day or two, if desired. If kept long enough, the yeast won't be as active so you won't get the same rise, but the pastry will still puff from the butter in the dough, just like puff pastry.

7. Refrigerate your finished pastries. They can be baked later in the day, the next day, or up to 2 days later.

ON BAKING DAY

1. Remove the pan from the refrigerator and heat the oven to 375°F.

2. Remove the plastic and brush the pastry with the egg wash. If you like, sprinkle the pastry with pearl sugar or granulated sugar. Bake the pastry until it's nicely browned, 30 to 35 minutes. Slide the parchment with the pastry on it onto a rack and let cool. When it's cool enough to handle, slide the pastry off the parchment. Serve at room temperature or chilled.

CHOCOLATE CROISSANTS

There are special chocolate sticks used for chocolate croissants, and while they make rolling the croissants a tiny bit easier, they aren't necessary at all. A good chocolate bar, chopped into small pieces, or even your favorite chocolate chips will work just as well.

Even though this is a sweet pastry and it includes chocolate, it's not super sweet, particularly if you choose a darker chocolate rather than semi-sweet.

The egg wash is optional, but I recommend it. It gives the pastry a nice shine and a little bit more of a crackly crust.

MAKES 8 CROISSANTS

ON PREP DAY 1

1. Whisk the yeast, sugar, milk, and egg in a medium bowl.

2. Put the flour, vanilla, and salt in a food processor and pulse a few times to distribute the salt. Cut the butter into a few pieces and put it in the food processor. Pulse until the butter pieces are no larger than a lima bean. It's fine if some pieces (or most of them) are smaller.

3. Transfer the flour-butter mixture to the bowl with the liquid. Stir gently until combined. The mixture will be wet, so don't worry if it seems loose. If it's not a wet mixture or if you are having trouble getting all the flour wet, drizzle in more milk, 1 tablespoon at a time, to moisten the dough. Cover the bowl and refrigerate overnight.

ON PREP DAY 2

1. Flour your work surface and turn out the dough. Flour the top of the dough, then pat it into a rough square. Using a rolling pin, roll the dough to about 18 inches square, though the shape doesn't matter so much. It could be the shape of Colorado. Well, Colorado would be ideal, but it's still fine if it looks like Nebraska. The point is to flatten the bits of butter that will make the buttery, flaky layers, but you don't want the butter to soften so much that it starts to mix with the flour, so work as quickly as possible. Flour your work surface and the top of the dough as needed to keep the dough from sticking.

2. Take the left third of the dough and fold it over the middle, then fold the right side over the middle, like you would fold a letter. Use a dough scraper under the dough to help lift it and fold it over. It's fine if the dough is sloppy and wants to break apart. Now, fold the top third down over the middle, then fold the bottom third up. You should have a fat square of dough.

continued

2¼ teaspoons active dry yeast

¼ cup sugar

¾ cup milk, plus more as needed

1 large egg

2½ cups (11¼ ounces) bread flour, plus more as needed

1 teaspoon pure vanilla extract

1 teaspoon kosher salt

2 sticks butter, cold (1 salted, 1 unsalted)

4 ounces dark chocolate, chopped

Egg wash (1 large egg beaten with 1 tablespoon water; optional)

3. Roll the dough to about 16 inches square, then fold following the same process as above. This time the dough should be easier to roll and fold.

4. Roll to 16 inches square one more time and fold as before. If at any time during the roll-and-fold process you feel that the butter is getting soft and squishy, put the dough in the refrigerator for 10 minutes or so to firm up the butter—you don't want it to mix with the flour.

5. Flour the dough, wrap it in plastic, and place it in a clean zip-top plastic bag. Refrigerate overnight or up to 2 days.

ON BAKING DAY

1. Line a baking sheet with parchment paper. Remove the dough from the refrigerator, divide it in half, rewrap half, and return it to the refrigerator.

2. Flour your work surface and roll the dough to about 10 x 18 inches, then cut it into four strips that are 4½ inches wide and 10 inches long.

3. Working with one strip at a time, place about ½ ounce of chocolate along the short end of a strip, then roll the strip up beginning at the end with the chocolate. Roll the strip gently, leaving room for the dough to puff up.

4. Place the finished pastries on the prepared baking sheet seam side down, leaving space between them to rise. Continue making pastries with the second half of the dough and the rest of the chocolate, or leave the dough refrigerated for another day.

5. Cover the pan with plastic wrap and set aside for 20 to 30 minutes. Meanwhile, heat the oven to 400°F. After 20 to 30 minutes, the dough won't seem to have risen, but it should feel puffy rather than firm.

6. Remove the plastic, brush the croissants with egg wash, if desired, and bake until nicely browned, 15 to 20 minutes. Transfer to a rack to cool before serving.

CINNAMON CROISSANTS

These sweet, buttery, cinnamon-flavored croissants will be the star of your breakfast or brunch table. They're particularly good with ham, and they're perfectly fine all by themselves with a cup of coffee, tea, or hot chocolate.

It will take you a few days from beginning to baking, but it's not a huge commitment of time at each step. And you can pause any time you need to—just refrigerate the dough and continue when you have time.

MAKES 16 CROISSANTS

ON PREP DAY 1

1. Make the cinnamon butter: Cut the butter into chunks. Place it in a food processor along with the brown sugar and cinnamon. Process until thoroughly mixed, scraping down the bowl as needed.

2. Transfer the butter to a zip-top plastic bag, flatten the butter into a fairly even layer in the bag, and place it in the freezer until fully chilled, at least 15 minutes, though you can do this well ahead of time, if you prefer.

3. Make the pastry: Whisk together the yeast, sugar, milk, and egg in a medium bowl.

4. Put the flour and salt in a food processor and pulse a few times to distribute the salt. Remove the cinnamon butter from the freezer, cut it into chunks, and put it in the food processor with the flour. Pulse until the butter pieces are no larger than a lima bean. It's fine if some pieces (or most of them) are smaller. This butter is softer than regular butter, so be careful not to blend it into the flour—you want discrete pieces to remain.

5. Transfer the flour-butter mixture to the bowl with the sugar-milk mixture. Stir very gently until combined. The mixture should be wet, so don't worry if it seems loose. If you mix it and see dry spots in the flour, drizzle in some water or milk, 1 tablespoon at a time, to moisten those spots.

6. Cover the bowl with plastic wrap and refrigerate overnight.

ON PREP DAY 2

1. Flour your work surface generously and turn out the dough. Flour the top of the dough, then pat it into a rough square. Using a rolling pin, roll the dough to about 18 inches square—it's fine if it's not an actual square. The point is to flatten the bits of butter that will make the buttery, flaky layers, but you don't want the butter

FOR THE CINNAMON BUTTER
2 sticks salted butter

2 tablespoons brown sugar

2 tablespoons ground cinnamon

FOR THE PASTRY
2$\frac{1}{4}$ teaspoons active dry yeast

2 tablespoons sugar

$\frac{3}{4}$ cup milk

1 large egg

2$\frac{1}{2}$ cups (9 ounces) bread flour, plus more as needed

1 teaspoon kosher salt

Egg wash (1 large egg beaten with 1 tablespoon water)

to soften so much that it starts to mix with the flour, so work as quickly as possible. Flour your work surface and the top of the dough as needed to keep the dough from sticking. You'll use more flour at the beginning of rolling than at the end.

2. Take the left third of the dough and fold it over the middle, then fold the right side over the middle, like you would fold a letter. Use a dough scraper under the dough to help lift it and fold it over. It's fine if the dough is sloppy and wants to break apart. Now, fold the top third down over the middle, then fold the bottom third up. You should have a fat square of dough.

3. Roll the dough to about 16 inches square, then perform the same folding process as above. This time the dough should be easier to roll and fold.

4. Once you have a fat square of dough, roll it one more time to 16 inches square and fold as before. If at any time during the rolling and folding you feel the butter getting soft and squishy, put the dough in the refrigerator for 10 minutes to firm up the butter. If the phone rings or you need to run an errand, simply refrigerate the dough at any point in the rolling and folding and continue when it's convenient, the same day or even a day later.

5. After the third roll-and-fold process, flour the dough, wrap it in plastic, and place it in a clean zip-top plastic bag. Refrigerate overnight or up to 2 days.

ON PREP DAY 3

1. Line two baking sheets with parchment paper (or use four quarter-sheet pans). Flour your work surface and divide the dough in half. Rewrap one piece and return it to the refrigerator.

2. Roll the first half into a disk about 14 inches in diameter. It's fine if it's not completely circular, but do the best you can. Cut the circle into 8 pie-shaped triangles.

3. Working with one triangle at a time, stretch the base to 6 inches wide and stretch the point to 9 inches long. This dough should stretch easily by hand, but if you prefer you can use a rolling pin.

4. Starting at the base of the triangle, roll the dough toward the point. Curve the roll into a crescent shape and place it on a prepared baking sheet.

5. Continue making croissants and placing them on the baking sheet, leaving room between them to rise. You should be able to fit 4 rolls on a quarter-sheet pan and 8 on a half-sheet pan. As you fill a pan, wrap it in plastic or place the whole pan in a large plastic bag and tie the open end shut. Let it rest at room temperature for at least 45 minutes, then refrigerate overnight.

continued

6. When you've finished with the first half of the dough, take the second piece out of the refrigerator and make croissants following the directions in Steps 2 through 4. Or, keep the unrolled dough refrigerated and make more rolls later or the next day.

ON BAKING DAY

1. Remove the pans from the refrigerator and heat the oven to 375°F.

2. Unwrap the pans and brush the croissants with the egg wash. Bake the rolls until they are nicely browned, about 25 minutes. Transfer the croissants to a wire rack to cool.

TIP

The cinnamon butter is softer than standard butter, so there's a tendency for it to mix into the dough. If you see that happening at any stage of the process, put the dough in the refrigerator to firm up.

Even if the butter mixes with the dough, all is not lost. You won't get the desired layers, but the flavor will still be good.

TRADITIONAL CROISSANTS

Making croissants the traditional way requires a lot of rolling the dough and letting it proof, but it's work that can be portioned out and done in small doses, like in between folding laundry or while you're waiting on hold for technical support.

The most important factor is to make sure the butter never melts, because once it has melted, it's never the same again. And if it gets so soft that it begins to incorporate into the flour, you'll lose the beautiful layers in the dough.

If you're making croissants in a hot kitchen in the summer, you might need to refrigerate the dough at every stage. If you're working in a cool room, you'll be able to work longer with less risk of melting butter.

While this is the most complicated recipe in this book, each step is easy enough to accomplish in a short amount of time, and the resting periods in between let you fit these luxurious pastries into your schedule. Do a little work, and pause for an hour or a day between steps—the dough will be patiently waiting for you.

MAKES 16 CROISSANTS

ON PREP DAY 1

1. Put the water, yeast, sugar, salt, flour, olive oil, dry milk, and egg in the bowl of a stand mixer fitted with the dough hook, and knead until a smooth dough forms. Or, mix in a large bowl and then knead by hand. Cover the bowl and let the dough rise at room temperature for 30 minutes, then refrigerate overnight or up to 24 hours. If it's more convenient, you can place the dough in a zip-top plastic bag rather than leaving it in the bowl.

2. Meanwhile, place the unwrapped butter sticks side by side in a gallon-size zip-top bag. Now (and this is the fun part!) use a rolling pin and pound on the butter to begin flattening it. First, you'll just make dents, but then you'll see that butter starts spreading a bit. Turn the bag over to attack from the other side, as well.

Once the butter is about half its original thickness, use the rolling pin to roll and flatten it. If you run into a solid bit, smack it with the rolling pin. Continue until you have a sheet of butter that's 10 inches square. Zip the top of the bag and refrigerate until needed.

continued

1¼ cups room temperature water

2¼ teaspoons active dry yeast

1 tablespoon sugar

2½ teaspoons kosher salt

3½ cups (15¾ ounces) bread flour, plus more as needed

2 tablespoons olive oil

½ cup nonfat dry milk

1 large egg

1 pound (4 sticks) unsalted butter

Egg wash (1 large egg beaten with 1 tablespoon water)

TIP

The butter you use does make a difference. You don't need to buy an artisanal butter, but it's worthwhile to spend just a little more for a brand name butter rather than a store brand. European butters are great but can be a bit pricey. Land O' Lakes and Challenge Butter are good domestic brands.

ON PREP DAY 2

1. Remove the dough from the refrigerator. Flour your work surface and turn out the dough. Roll it to a 16-inch square.

2. Take the butter out of the refrigerator and remove it from the bag (it's easiest to cut the bag and peel it away from the butter). Place the butter on top of the dough so that the corners of the butter are pointing toward the sides of the dough, leaving you with four triangular flaps.

3. Fold the triangular flaps of dough neatly over the butter to form a new square with the butter fully enclosed by the dough. With your rolling pin, roll the dough to form an 18-inch square.

4. Take the left third of the dough and fold it over the middle, then fold the right side over the middle, like you would fold a letter. Now, fold the top third down over the middle, then fold the bottom third up. You should have a fat square of dough. If at any time during the rolling and folding you feel the butter getting soft and squishy, put the dough in the refrigerator for 10 minutes to firm up the butter—you don't want it to mix with the dough. If the phone rings or you need to run an errand, simply refrigerate the dough at any point in the rolling and folding and continue when it's convenient, the same day or even a day later.

5. Roll the dough to about 18 inches square again, then fold following the same process as above. Wrap the dough in plastic wrap and refrigerate for at least 20 minutes to firm up the butter. You can let it rest longer—several hours or even the next day. If you're going to leave it more than a few hours, put the wrapped dough in a plastic bag. The dough will begin to rise, and any that escapes the plastic wrap will dry out on the surface.

6. After the dough has rested and chilled, roll it to 18 inches square one more time and fold as before. Wrap the dough again, and refrigerate for a minimum of 20 minutes. Again, you can also let it rest several hours or until the next day— whatever is convenient for you.

WHEN YOU'RE READY TO FORM THE CROISSANTS

1. Line two or three baking sheets with parchment paper. Remove the dough from the refrigerator and divide the dough evenly into 2 rectangular pieces. Rewrap 1 piece and put it back into the refrigerator while you work on the other piece.

2. Using your rolling pin, roll the dough to a 10 x 20-inch rectangle. Cut the rectangle in half, so you have two 10-inch squares. Now, cut one of the squares to form 4 triangles.

3. Working with 1 triangular piece at a time, stretch the dough. Choose one cut side to be the base of the triangle, with the point opposite the base. Stretch the base to about 7 inches wide, then pull and stretch the length from the base to the point to about 9 inches. The dough should stretch easily. With the base of the triangle facing you, roll it up toward the point. Place the finished roll on a baking sheet with the point underneath and form the dough into a curved crescent shape. Continue in the same fashion with the rest of the dough, making sure you leave plenty of room between the rolls for them to rise.

4. Once a baking sheet is full (6 rolls is plenty) cover it with plastic wrap. Let the sheet rest at room temperature for 20 minutes, then refrigerate. You can bake these later the same day or up to 2 days later. If you want to bake the croissants immediately, let them rise until they feel soft and puffy, about 45 minutes total, then follow the baking instructions.

ON BAKING DAY

1. Remove the pan from the refrigerator and let the croissants rest at room temperature or in a slightly warm—but not hot—location while the oven heats to 375°F. You'll get the puffiest result if you let the croissants come to room temperature before baking—the dough will feel soft rather than hard, as it does when it first emerges from the refrigerator. If you bake sooner, you'll still have good croissants, but they won't expand quite as much.

2. Remove the plastic wrap and brush the croissants with the egg wash. Bake the croissants until they are golden-brown, about 25 minutes. Transfer the croissants to a rack to cool. Serve slightly warm or at room temperature.

FETA, ROSEMARY, *and* SUN-DRIED TOMATO TURNOVERS

These turnovers make a great light lunch paired with a salad or fruit.

When shopping for sun-dried tomatoes, you have many choices, from tomatoes packed in oil, to soft, squishy tomatoes you'll find near the dried fruits, to tomatoes that are completely dry.

I like the soft, squishy tomatoes, which have a vibrant red color, don't taste quite as cooked, and still have some of their bright flavor. The darker leathery tomatoes have a deeper, sweeter flavor. Any sun-dried tomatoes will work, so choose the one you like best.

If you're using tomatoes packed in oil, drain as much oil as possible and reduce the cooking oil by about a tablespoon to compensate. The filling should be moist but not greasy.

MAKES 18 TURNOVERS

ON PREP DAY 1

1. Make the filling: Put the olive oil and butter in a medium sauté pan and heat on medium until the butter melts. Add the onions and rosemary and cook until the onions soften and become translucent, about 5 minutes. Add the tomatoes and black pepper. Continue cooking until the tomatoes soften, about 5 more minutes. Test an onion—it should be cooked through with no onion "bite."

2. Transfer the mixture to a storage container and refrigerate. When the mixture is chilled (about 40 minutes), mix in the feta, then refrigerate until needed for the pastry. The filling can be made ahead, or prepared the day you bake, but it should be fully chilled before it is used to fill the pastry.

3. Make the pastry: Whisk the yeast, water, egg, and sugar in a medium bowl.

4. Put the flour and salt in a food processor and pulse a few times to distribute the salt. Cut the butter into a few pieces and put it in the food processor. Pulse until the butter pieces are no larger than a lima bean. It's fine if some pieces (or most of them) are smaller.

5. Transfer the flour-butter mixture to the bowl with the liquid. Stir gently until combined. The mixture will be wet, so don't worry if it seems loose. If it's not a wet mixture or if you are having trouble getting all the flour wet, drizzle in more water, 1 tablespoon at a time. Cover the bowl and refrigerate overnight.

ON PREP DAY 2

1. Flour your work surface and turn out the dough. Flour the top of the dough, then pat it into a rough square. Using a rolling pin, roll the dough to about 18 inches square, though the shape doesn't matter so much. The point is to flatten the bits of

continued

FOR THE FILLING

1 tablespoon olive oil

1 tablespoon unsalted butter

1 large onion, cut into large dice

$1/2$ teaspoon dried rosemary

3 ounces sun-dried tomatoes, chopped roughly (if using jarred tomatoes, be sure to drain well)

Several grinds black pepper

4 ounces feta cheese, crumbled

FOR THE PASTRY

$2 1/4$ teaspoons active dry yeast

$3/4$ cup room temperature water, plus more as needed

1 large egg

1 tablespoon sugar

$2 1/2$ cups ($11 1/4$ ounces) bread flour, plus more as needed

1 teaspoon kosher salt

2 sticks butter (1 salted, 1 unsalted)

Egg wash (1 large egg beaten with 1 tablespoon water; optional)

butter that will make the buttery, flaky layers, but you don't want the butter to soften so much that it starts to mix with the flour, so work as quickly as possible. Flour your work surface and the top of the dough as needed to keep the dough from sticking.

2. Take the left third of the dough and fold it over the middle, then fold the right side over the middle, like you would fold a letter. Use a dough scraper under the dough to help lift it and fold it over. It's fine if the dough is sloppy and wants to break apart. Now, fold the top third down over the middle, then fold the bottom third up. You should have a fat square of dough.

3. Roll the dough to about 16 inches square, and perform the same folding process. This time the dough should be easier to roll and fold.

4. Roll the dough to about 16 inches square, then fold following the same process as above.

5. Roll to 16 inches square one more time and fold as before. If at any time during the roll-and-fold process you feel that the butter is getting soft and squishy, put the dough in the refrigerator for 10 minutes or so to firm up the butter—you don't want it to mix with the flour.

6. Flour the dough, wrap it in plastic, and place it in a clean zip-top plastic bag. Refrigerate overnight or up to 2 days.

ON BAKING DAY

1. Line a baking sheet with parchment paper. Remove the dough from the refrigerator, divide it in half, rewrap half of the dough, and return it to the refrigerator.

2. Flour your work surface and roll the dough to 12 inches square. Cut the dough into three 4-inch rows both horizontally and vertically so you end up with 9 even squares (each about 4 x 4 inches).

3. Spoon a generous teaspoon of the filling into the center of each square. You should use up about half of the filling.

4. Put some water in a small bowl and use your finger or a pastry brush to lightly moisten the edges of the squares. Fold each square into a triangle—you'll need to stretch the dough a bit to cover the filling. Press a fork along the joined edges of the pastry to help seal it. Place the filled pastries on the prepared baking sheet, leaving space between them to rise. Continue making pastries with the second half of the dough and rest of the filling, or leave the dough refrigerated for another day.

5. Cover the pan with plastic wrap and set aside for 20 to 30 minutes. Meanwhile, heat the oven to 400°F. After 20 to 30 minutes, the dough won't seem to have risen, but it should feel puffy rather than firm.

6. Remove the plastic and brush the top of the turnovers with egg wash (if using). Use a sharp knife to cut a few slits in the top of the pastries. Bake the turnovers until they're nicely browned, 15 to 20 minutes. Transfer to a rack to cool before serving.

APPLE CHAI TURNOVERS

The flavor in these turnovers is unexpected, with the chai mix adding spice and dairy notes to the apples. Of course, if you're not a fan of chai, you could simply add cinnamon or vanilla to the apples, as you would for apple pie. If you want to eliminate a step, you can use your favorite prepared pie filling.

If you use fresh apples, look for those that are good for pies and baking so they keep their shape; otherwise, you'll end up with something that's the consistency of applesauce. Granny Smiths are a good choice.

MAKES 18 TURNOVERS

ON PREP DAY 1

1. Make the filling: Melt the butter in a sauté pan and add the apples, chai mix, salt, and about 1 tablespoon sugar. Cook on medium heat, stirring as needed, until the apples soften a bit, 3 to 4 minutes. Taste and add more sugar to your liking. Continue cooking until most of the moisture in the pan is gone and the remaining liquid is thick and syrupy, about 5 minutes. Transfer the filling to a storage container and refrigerate until needed. You can make this up to 2 days in advance or just before it is needed. Be sure you allow enough time for it to cool.

2. Make the pastry: Whisk the yeast, egg, milk, honey, and crème fraîche in a medium bowl.

3. Put the flour and salt in a food processor and pulse a few times to distribute the salt. Cut the butter into a few pieces and put it in the food processor. Pulse until the butter pieces are no larger than a lima bean. It's fine if some pieces (or most of them) are smaller.

4. Transfer the flour-butter mixture to the bowl with the liquid. Stir gently until combined. The mixture will be wet, so don't worry if it seems loose. If it's not a wet mixture or if you are having trouble getting all the flour wet, drizzle in more milk, 1 tablespoon at a time, to moisten the dough. Cover the bowl and refrigerate overnight. You can also transfer the dough to a zip-top plastic bag for refrigerating, if that's more convenient.

ON PREP DAY 2

1. Flour your work surface and turn out the dough. Flour the top of the dough, then pat it into a rough square. Using a rolling pin, roll the dough to about 18 inches square, though the shape doesn't matter so much. The point is to flatten the bits of butter that will make the buttery, flaky layers, but you don't want the

continued

FOR THE FILLING

1 tablespoon unsalted butter

4 large or 5 medium apples, peeled, cored, and cut into ¼-inch cubes

¼ cup powdered instant chai mix

½ teaspoon kosher salt

¼ cup sugar

FOR THE PASTRY

2¼ teaspoons active dry yeast

1 large egg

¾ cup milk, plus more as needed

1 tablespoon honey

¼ cup crème fraîche

2½ cups (11¼ ounces) bread flour, plus more as needed

1 teaspoon kosher salt

2 sticks cold butter (1 salted, 1 unsalted)

Egg wash (1 large egg beaten with 1 tablespoon water; optional)

butter to soften so much that it starts to mix with the flour, so work as quickly as possible. Flour your work surface and the top of the dough as needed to keep the dough from sticking.

2. Take the left third of the dough and fold it over the middle, then fold the right side over the middle, like you would fold a letter. Use a dough scraper under the dough to help lift it and fold it over. It's fine if the dough is sloppy and wants to break apart. Now, fold the top third over the middle, then fold the bottom third up. You should have a fat square of dough.

3. Roll the dough to about 16 inches square, and perform the same folding process. This time the dough should be easier to roll and fold.

4. Roll to 16 inches square one more time and fold as before. If at any time during the roll-and-fold process you feel that the butter is getting soft and squishy, put the dough in the refrigerator for 10 minutes or so to firm up the butter—you don't want it to mix with the flour. It's fine to refrigerate the dough at any point in the rolling and folding process and then continue when it's convenient—the same day or even a day later.

5. Flour the dough, wrap it in plastic, and place it in a clean zip-top plastic bag. Refrigerate overnight or up to 2 days.

ON PREP DAY 3

1. Line two baking sheets with parchment paper. Remove the dough from the refrigerator, divide it in half, rewrap half of the dough, and return it to the refrigerator.

2. Flour your work surface and roll the dough to 12 inches square. Cut the dough in a tic-tac-toe pattern into 9 even squares (each about 4 x 4 inches).

3. Spoon a generous teaspoon of the filling into the center of each square. You should use up about half of the filling.

4. Put some water in a small bowl and use your finger or a pastry brush to lightly moisten the edges of the squares. Fold each square into a triangle—you'll need to stretch the dough a bit to cover the filling. Press a fork along the joined edges of the pastry to help seal it. Place the filled pastries on the prepared baking sheets, leaving space between them, to rise. Continue making pastries with the second half of the dough and rest of the filling, or leave the dough refrigerated for another day.

5. Cover the pans with plastic wrap and let sit at room temperature for 20 minutes. You can bake the pastries immediately or refrigerate them for up to 2 days and bake them later.

ON BAKING DAY

1. If your pastries were refrigerated after forming, remove them from the refrigerator and let them rest while the oven heats to 375°F.

2. Remove the plastic. The dough, whether refrigerated or not, won't seem to have risen, but it should feel puffy rather than firm. Brush the pastries with egg wash, if desired, then use a sharp knife to cut a few slits in the tops.

3. Bake the pastries until nicely browned, about 20 minutes. Transfer to a wire rack and cool.

TIP

If you've purchased heavy cream for a recipe and have extra, making crème fraîche is one way to preserve the cream for a little longer than it would normally last. Since crème fraîche is soured in a good way, it thwarts the growth of bad bacteria that would ruin your fresh cream.

To make crème fraîche at home, just put $1/2$ cup of buttermilk in a pint jar, fill with heavy cream, stir, and cover. Leave the jar at room temperature until it thickens; depending on your room temperature, this will likely take 8 hours or longer. Refrigerate tightly covered. Homemade crème fraîche will keep for about a week.

PINEAPPLE SWEET CHEESE DANISH

A large Danish pastry makes a very pretty presentation when it's served whole, but even the slices are attractive, with visible layers of pastry, cheese, and pineapple and the pearl sugar decorating the top.

The pearl sugar isn't required, but it's a lovely garnish. Unlike sugar crystals, pearl sugar is white, round, and sort of puffy. It doesn't melt on top of the pastry, and it stays bright white to provide contrast against the browned pastry.

This is a long recipe, with several steps over several days, but each day's work isn't very time-consuming. The result is well worth the effort.

MAKES TWO 7 X 14-INCH PASTRIES

ON PREP DAY 1

1. Make the filling: Combine the ricotta, cream cheese, sugar, and lemon zest in a small bowl. Mix well, making sure the cream cheese and ricotta are thoroughly blended. Refrigerate until needed.

2. Make the pastry: Whisk the yeast, milk, egg, and sugar in a medium bowl.

3. Put the flour and salt in a food processor and pulse a few times to distribute the salt. Cut the butter into a few pieces and put it in the food processor. Pulse until the butter pieces are no larger than a lima bean. It's fine if some pieces (or most of them) are smaller.

4. Transfer the flour-butter mixture to the bowl with the liquid. Stir gently until combined. The mixture will be wet, so don't worry if it seems loose. If it's not a wet mixture or if you are having trouble getting all the flour wet, drizzle in more milk, 1 tablespoon at a time, to moisten the dough. Cover the bowl and refrigerate overnight.

ON PREP DAY 2

1. Flour your work surface and turn out the dough. Flour the top of the dough, then pat it into a rough square. Using a rolling pin, roll the dough to about 18 inches square, though the shape doesn't matter so much. The point is to flatten the bits of butter that will make the buttery, flaky layers, but you don't want the butter to soften so much that it starts to mix with the flour, so work as quickly as possible. Flour your work surface and the top of the dough as needed to keep the dough from sticking.

continued

FOR THE FILLING

1 cup (8 ounces) ricotta cheese

4 ounces cream cheese, at room temperature

2 tablespoons sugar

Zest of $\frac{1}{2}$ lemon

One 20-ounce can crushed pineapple, well drained

FOR THE PASTRY

2 $\frac{1}{4}$ teaspoons active dry yeast

$\frac{3}{4}$ cup milk, plus more as needed

1 large egg

$\frac{1}{4}$ cup sugar

2 $\frac{1}{2}$ cups (11$\frac{1}{4}$ ounces) bread flour, plus more as needed

1 teaspoon kosher salt

2 sticks butter, cold (1 salted, 1 unsalted)

Egg wash (1 large egg beaten with 1 tablespoon water; optional)

Pearl sugar, for sprinkling (optional)

2. Take the left third of the dough and fold it over the middle, then fold the right side over the middle, like you would fold a letter. Use a dough scraper under the dough to help lift it and fold it over. It's fine if the dough is sloppy and wants to break apart. Now, fold the top third down over the middle, then fold the bottom third up. You should have a fat square of dough.

3. Roll the dough to about 16 inches square, and perform the same folding process. This time the dough should be easier to roll and fold.

4. Roll to 16 inches square one more time and fold as before. If at any time during the roll-and-fold process you feel that the butter is getting soft and squishy, put the dough in the refrigerator for 10 minutes or so to firm up the butter—you don't want it to mix with the flour.

5. Flour the dough, wrap it in plastic, and place it in a clean zip-top plastic bag. Refrigerate overnight or up to 2 days.

ON PREP DAY 3

1. Remove the dough from the refrigerator, divide it in half, rewrap half and return it to the refrigerator.

2. Flour your work surface and roll the dough to 9 x 16 inches. Transfer it to a piece of parchment paper that will fit a baking sheet.

3. Spread half of the cheese mixture lengthwise down the middle third of the dough, leaving about an inch uncovered on the two short ends. Spread half of the drained pineapple on top of the cheese mixture.

Now it's decision time. You can simply fold the uncovered dough on top of the filling for a very simple presentation, or you can opt for a braided look. If you don't braid, the dough will spread widthwise quite a bit, but if you braid, it will stay more compact and be a bit taller. You've got a second piece of dough and more filling, so you can make one of each.

4. If you opt for the simple version, fold the short ends toward the middle first, leaving about an inch of filling between the edges. Then fold the long sides over, leaving about an inch of filling peeking through in the middle. This gap will widen significantly during baking. Press the dough together at the corners to keep the pastry from flopping open during baking. Slide the parchment, with the pastry on it, onto a sheet pan. Nudge and adjust the pastry as needed to straighten it. Cover the pastry with plastic wrap and set aside for 20 to 30 minutes.

5. If you decide to braid, use a sharp knife, pizza cutter, or pastry cutter to cut slits from the edge of the dough to within about 1/2 inch of the filling along both long sides, leaving about 1 inch between the slits. This creates strips that will be folded over the filled center of the dough. To start the folding process, first fold over the two short ends so they just cover the filling. Then begin folding the strips from the edges over the center of the dough, alternating strips from one side of the pastry and

then the other and letting them overlap in the center. The dough will stretch quite easily to allow you to do this. Flatten out any creases as you fold the strips so they lay flat. While you're not actually braiding, you will end up with a braided effect. Slide the parchment, with the pastry on it, onto a sheet pan, then nudge and tuck where needed to straighten the pastry. Cover the pastry with plastic wrap and set aside for 20 to 30 minutes.

6. Make a second Danish from the reserved dough, or keep that dough for another day or two, if desired. If kept long enough, the yeast won't be as active so you won't get the same rise, but the pastry will still puff from the butter in the dough, just like puff pastry.

7. Refrigerate your finished pastries. They can be baked later in the day, the next day, or up to 2 days later.

ON BAKING DAY

1. Remove the pan from the refrigerator and heat the oven to 400°F.

2. Remove the plastic. The dough won't seem to have risen, but it should feel puffy rather than firm. Brush the Danish with egg wash and sprinkle with the pearl sugar, if using. Bake the pastry until nicely browned, 30 to 35 minutes, rotating the pans halfway through baking. Transfer the pastry on parchment to a rack to cool; serve warm, at room temperature, or chilled.

BREAKFAST SAUSAGE DANISH

Most Danish recipes are sweet, but this savory version incorporates breakfast sausage, so it's great for breakfast, brunch, or lunch. Because of the sausage, it's best served warm or at room temperature, but if you're a fan of cold pizza, you might appreciate this chilled.

MAKES TWO 7 X 14-INCH PASTRIES

ON PREP DAY 1

1. Make the filling: In a medium sauté pan over medium heat, cook the sausage, bell pepper, onions, and sage, stirring as needed, until the vegetables are cooked through and there's no pink left in the meat, 5 to 6 minutes. Drain off any excess fat or moisture, then refrigerate until chilled. Mix in the shredded Jack cheese. You can make the filling up to 2 days ahead and keep it refrigerated, or make it when needed; just be sure to allow enough time for it to chill.

2. Make the pastry: Whisk the yeast, milk, egg, and sugar in a medium bowl.

3. Put the flour and salt in a food processor and pulse a few times to distribute the salt. Cut the butter into a few pieces and put it in the food processor. Pulse until the butter pieces are no larger than a lima bean. It's fine if some pieces (or most of them) are smaller.

4. Transfer the flour-butter mixture to the bowl with the liquid, then add the shredded Cheddar. Stir gently until combined. The mixture will be wet, so don't worry if it seems loose. If it's not a wet mixture or if you are having trouble getting all the flour wet, add more milk, 1 tablespoon at a time, to moisten the dough. Cover the bowl and refrigerate overnight.

ON PREP DAY 2

1. Flour your work surface and turn out the dough. Flour the top of the dough, then pat it into a rough square. Using a rolling pin, roll the dough to about 18 inches square, though the shape doesn't matter so much. The point is to flatten the bits of butter that will make the buttery, flaky layers, but you don't want the butter to soften so much that it starts to mix with the flour, so work as quickly as possible. Flour your work surface and the top of the dough as needed to keep the dough from sticking.

2. Take the left third of the dough and fold it over the middle, then fold the right side over the middle, like you would fold a letter. Use a dough scraper under the dough to help lift it and fold it over. It's fine if the dough is sloppy and wants to break apart. Now, fold the top third down over the middle, then fold the bottom third up. You should have a fat square of dough.

3. Roll the dough to about 16 inches square, and perform the same folding process. This time the dough should be easier to roll and fold.

FOR THE FILLING

1 pound bulk breakfast sausage

1/2 large green bell pepper, cut into small dice

1 medium onion, diced

1 teaspoon dried sage

4 ounces Monterey Jack cheese, shredded

FOR THE PASTRY

2 1/4 teaspoons active dry yeast

1 cup milk, plus more as needed

1 large egg

1 tablespoon sugar

2 1/2 cups (11 1/4 ounces) bread flour, plus more as needed

1 teaspoon kosher salt

2 sticks unsalted butter

2 ounces mild Cheddar cheese, shredded

Egg wash (1 large egg beaten with 1 tablespoon water)

4. Roll to 16 inches square one more time and fold as before. If at any time during the roll-and-fold process you feel that the butter is getting soft and squishy, put the dough in the refrigerator for 10 minutes or so to firm up the butter—you don't want it to mix with the flour. It's fine to refrigerate the dough at any point in the rolling and folding process and then continue when it's convenient—the same day or even a day later.

5. Flour the dough, wrap it in plastic, and place it in a clean zip-top plastic bag. Refrigerate overnight or up to 2 days.

ON PREP DAY 3

1. Remove the dough from the refrigerator, divide it in half, rewrap half of the dough, and return it to the refrigerator.

2. Flour your work surface and roll the dough to 9 x 16 inches. Transfer it to a piece of parchment paper that will fit a baking sheet.

3. Spread half of the meat and cheese mixture lengthwise down the middle third of the dough, leaving about an inch uncovered on the two short ends.

4. Using a sharp knife, pizza cutter, or pastry cutter, cut slits from the edge of the dough to within about 1/2 inch of the filling along both long sides, leaving about 1 inch between the slits. This creates strips that will be folded over the filled center.

5. To start the folding process, first fold over the two short ends so they just cover the filling. Then begin folding the strips from the edges over the center of the dough, alternating strips from one side of the pastry and then the other and letting them overlap in the center. The dough will stretch quite easily to allow you to do this. Flatten out any creases as you fold the strips so they lay flat. While you're not actually braiding, you will end up with a braided effect. Slide the parchment, with the pastry on it, onto a baking sheet, then nudge and tuck where needed to straighten the pastry. Cover the pastry with plastic wrap and set aside for 20 minutes.

6. Make a second Danish from the reserved dough, or keep that dough for another day or two, if desired. If kept long enough, the yeast won't be as active so you won't get the same rise, but the pastry will still puff from the butter in the dough, just like puff pastry.

7. Refrigerate your finished pastries. They can be baked later in the day or the next day.

ON BAKING DAY

1. Remove the pan from the refrigerator and heat the oven to 375°F.

2. Remove the plastic and brush the pastry with the egg wash. Bake the pastry until nicely browned, 30 to 35 minutes. Slide the parchment with the pastry on it onto a rack and let cool. Serve warm or at room temperature.

TIP

If you can't find bulk breakfast sausage, buy patties and break them up, or buy link sausages and remove the casings. You could also make this with any other sausage you like. Italian sausage would be wonderful (eliminate the sage from the filling), served with marinara on the side.

LEFTOVER BREAD

ALMOND BUTTER BREAD PUDDING

My first few experiences with bread pudding were less than exciting. Then I tried one that was rich and custardy, and I fell in love. To me, bread pudding is a dessert, and it should be rich. While it's certainly related to its savory cousin, the strata, it's also related to French toast and custards.

You can cook this without the water bath, but the water makes it a little more foolproof—you'll get a custardy interior, a crisp top, and a great dessert.

Try this recipe with leftover Cinnamon Swirl Bread (p. 48) or Maple Sugar and Candied Walnut Swirl Bread (p. 55), as well as any of the unflavored white or wheat breads.

SERVES 4

1. Heat the oven to 325°F.

2. Combine the milk, eggs, cream, sugar, almond butter, and vanilla extract in a medium bowl. Whisk until combined. It's fine if the almond butter remains in lumps, but the rest should be well combined.

3. Add the bread cubes to the bowl and stir. Let them sit for a few moments to absorb the liquid. Portion the bread and liquid into four 1-cup ramekins or an 8-inch square baking pan. You can cook this immediately or cover and refrigerate; the bread will absorb more liquid the longer you wait.

4. If using ramekins, place them in a casserole dish or baking pan and fill the pan with hot, nearly boiling water to about halfway up the sides of the ramekins. Place the pan in the oven and bake until the puddings puff up and a knife inserted in the center comes out mostly clean, about 50 minutes. If cooking in an 8-inch pan, bake for 50 minutes as well and check for doneness. It's fine if there's a bit of almond or a bit of cooked custard on the knife, but it shouldn't be wet and liquidy.

5. Carefully remove the ramekins from the hot water, if using, and serve warm.

1 cup milk

4 large eggs

$1/2$ cup heavy cream

$1/2$ cup sugar

$1/2$ cup almond butter

1 tablespoon pure vanilla extract

4 cups $1/2$-inch bread cubes

ARTICHOKE, OLIVE, *and* SUN-DRIED TOMATO STRATA

This is fancy enough for a festive lunch or brunch, but it's simple and takes advantage of leftover bread. The strata needs to rest for several hours to let the bread completely absorb the egg mixture, so it's a great make-ahead dish, especially when entertaining. Just take it out of the refrigerator, pop it into the oven, and set a timer.

Make this strata with any of the white or wheat breads or try it with leftover Three Cheese Bread with Kalamata Olives (p. 40) or the Tomato and Black Olive Bread (p. 42).

SERVES 4

1. In a 1-quart casserole, put half of the bread cubes in an even layer on the bottom. Add half of the artichoke hearts, half of the tomatoes, and half of the olives, sprinkling them evenly over the bread. Add the remaining bread cubes and then the remaining artichoke hearts, tomatoes, and olives.

2. In a medium bowl, whisk the milk, eggs, salt, and pepper, then pour evenly over the top of the casserole. Sprinkle the cheese on top.

3. Cover the casserole with plastic wrap and refrigerate overnight or up to 24 hours.

4. When you're ready to bake, remove the plastic from the pan; place the pan in a cold oven and heat it to 325°F. Cook until a knife inserted in the center of the strata comes out clean (it can be a little damp, but there shouldn't be wet egg mixture clinging to it), about 1 hour 15 minutes. Or, cook in a preheated 325°F oven for 1 hour 10 minutes. (If you're cooking in a glass or ceramic pan, place it on a baking sheet to reduce the chance it will crack from thermal shock as it goes from refrigerator temperature to hot oven.)

5. Let the strata rest for 5 to 10 minutes to allow the eggs to set. Cut and serve warm or at room temperature.

---

4 cups $1/2$- to $3/4$-inch crouton-size bread cubes

One 14-ounce can artichoke hearts, halved or quartered

$1/4$ cup sun-dried tomatoes, chopped or julienned

$1/4$ cup sliced Kalamata olives

1 cup milk

5 large eggs

1 teaspoon kosher salt

$1/2$ teaspoon white pepper

3 ounces Monterey Jack cheese, shredded

TIP

Look for the smallest artichoke hearts you can find—the larger ones tend to have tough outer leaves, and there's nothing much worse than biting into one of those inedible pieces. While you're halving (or quartering) the artichoke hearts, look for those tough outer leaves and remove them.

If you can find frozen artichoke hearts, give them a try. They taste fresher than the canned variety.

CHERRY *and* GOAT CHEESE STRATA

Dried cherries pack a huge flavor punch. There are several types available, so choose sweet or tart to change the taste of this strata. Meanwhile, the goat cheese adds richness and offsets the tartness of the cherries if you use that variety.

For a different look, you could chop the cherries into little bits and mix them with the bread rather than keeping them in a single layer along with the cheese.

This strata is delicious with leftover Rich Egg and Butter Loaf (p. 21), sourdough, or any white or wheat bread. For extra cherry punch, you could also use the Oatmeal-Cherry-Walnut Loaf (p. 58).

SERVES 4

1. Whisk the eggs, buttermilk, sugar, and salt in a medium bowl.

2. Place about half of the bread cubes in the bottom of a 1-quart casserole. Put dots of chèvre on top of the bread, then sprinkle the cherries on top. Add the rest of the bread cubes.

3. Pour the egg mixture evenly on top of the bread. Press the mixture down a bit to make sure all the bread is moistened, then cover the casserole with plastic wrap and refrigerate overnight or up to 24 hours.

4. When you're ready to bake, remove the plastic from the pan; place the pan in a cold oven and heat it to 325°F. (If you're cooking in a glass or ceramic pan, place it on a baking sheet to reduce the chance it will crack from thermal shock as it goes from refrigerator temperature to hot oven.) Cook until a knife inserted in the center of the strata comes out clean (it can be a little damp, but there shouldn't be wet egg mixture clinging to it), about 1 hour 15 minutes. Or, cook in a preheated 325°F oven for 1 hour 10 minutes.

5. Let the strata rest for 5 to 10 minutes to allow the eggs to set. Cut and serve warm or at room temperature.

4 large eggs
$1/2$ cup buttermilk
1 tablespoon sugar
1 teaspoon kosher salt
4 cups bread cubes
4 ounces chèvre (goat cheese)
$1/4$ cup dried cherries

TIP

You can use other dried fruits if you're not fond of cherries. Try apples or cranberries.

APPLE PIE BREAD PUDDING

If you like warm apple pie, you'll love this bread pudding. Top it with some whipped cream or a small scoop of vanilla ice cream and a drizzle of caramel sauce for an over-the-top dessert.

Any white or wheat bread would work for this recipe, but the Cinnamon Swirl Bread (p. 48) and Maple Sugar Fans (p. 109) are really delicious. I've even used dinner rolls and burger buns. If you have leftover sweet breads, those are nice too, as long as you like the flavor combinations.

SERVES 4

1. Heat the oven to 325°F.

2. Melt the butter in a sauté pan and add the apples. Cook until they start to soften, about 5 minutes, then remove from the heat.

3. In a medium bowl, whisk the milk, cream, eggs, vanilla, cinnamon, sugar, and salt. Add the apples and bread cubes and stir to combine. Let the mixture sit for a few minutes so the bread can absorb the liquid. Portion the mixture into four 1-cup ramekins. You can cook immediately or cover and refrigerate; the bread will absorb more liquid the longer you wait.

4. Place the ramekins in a casserole dish or baking pan and fill the pan with hot, nearly boiling water to about halfway up the sides of the ramekins. Place the pan in the oven and bake until the puddings puff up and a knife inserted in the center of a ramekin comes out mostly clean, about 50 minutes. It's fine if there's a bit of cooked custard on the knife, but it shouldn't be wet and liquidy.

5. Carefully remove the ramekins from the hot water and serve warm.

1 tablespoon unsalted butter

2 baking apples (I like Granny Smith), peeled, cored, and cut into $1/4$-inch dice

1 cup milk

$1/4$ cup heavy cream

4 large eggs

1 tablespoon pure vanilla extract

1 teaspoon ground cinnamon

$1/2$ cup sugar

$1/2$ teaspoon kosher salt

4 cups bread cubes

TIP

For even more cinnamon flavor, sprinkle a little cinnamon sugar (2 parts sugar to 1 part cinnamon) on top of the bread puddings before you bake them. For crunch, top with finely chopped walnuts or pecans.

HERBED CROUTONS

Why buy croutons when you can make your own? Some folks prefer croutons that are made from the inside of the bread—no crust—but if you're making your own bread, that crust is probably very toasty and tasty, so I suggest you use all of the bread, including the ends.

You can turn just about any leftover bread into croutons, even the sweet or flavored ones. The exception would be bread with fillings that could burn, like the jam-filled ones.

Keep the bread flavors in mind when seasoning your croutons. You might not want any seasonings at all if the bread is highly seasoned. Besides seasoning your croutons with herbs and spices, consider flavored oils, like basil oil, lemon oil, or chive oil. Of course, you can season the croutons to match what you're serving or what you like. Try garlic powder, paprika, marjoram, poultry seasoning, or Greek, Italian, Mexican, or Cajun seasoning blends—or anything else you like.

MAKES 8 CUPS

1. Heat the oven to 250°F.

2. Put the bread cubes in a large bowl and drizzle with the olive oil, stirring or tossing the cubes to get the oil as evenly distributed as possible. Add the herbs one at a time, tossing the cubes to incorporate. Season with salt and pepper.

3. Spread the bread cubes on a baking sheet in an even layer. Bake until the cubes are completely dry and crisp and just beginning to get toasted. How long it takes depends on the bread you're using, but start checking after 15 minutes. If the cubes aren't cooking evenly you might need to stir them around in the pan a bit.

4. Let the cubes cool on the pan, then transfer to a storage container or zip-top plastic bag.

8 cups $\frac{1}{2}$-inch plain bread cubes

2 tablespoons olive oil

1 teaspoon dried oregano

1 teaspoon dried thyme

$\frac{1}{4}$ teaspoon dried sage

$\frac{1}{4}$ teaspoon dried powdered rosemary

Kosher salt and black pepper

TIP

Croutons, like commercial crackers or crisp breadsticks, have a long shelf life because completely dry bread is unlikely to get moldy. However, they don't last forever, so make them with a plan for using them. Most folks add them to salads, but I like them for snacking.

FOUR CHEESE STRATA

While some stratas are planned in advance and carefully shopped for, I suspect that some are created based on what's left in the refrigerator—eggs, cream, some bits of cheese.

This is a very cheesy version, like a bread-based version of mac and cheese. But it's not just for breakfast or brunch. Serve it for lunch with a salad or for dinner as a side dish. This strata makes good use of leftover rye bread, the Three Cheese Bread with Kalamata Olives (p. 40), or even the Stuffing Bread with Dried Cranberries (p. 38).

You can change the cheeses, but make sure they go together well. Choose your favorite or use up the bits you have in the fridge. I suggest you have at least one yellow cheese, for the color. Fire-roasted red peppers, chunks of ham, or roasted vegetables would make tasty additions to this strata.

SERVES 4

1. Spray a 9 x 5-inch loaf pan with cooking spray or brush with butter.

2. Combine the cream cheese, eggs, Parmesan, and heavy cream in a large bowl; whisk to combine. It's fine if the cream cheese doesn't smooth out completely and small bits remain, but you don't want large pieces.

3. Put one layer of the bread cubes in the bottom of the pan (to help keep the cheese off the bottom of the pan). Place the remaining bread cubes in the bowl with the egg mixture. Add the cubed cheeses and mix well.

4. Transfer the mixture to the loaf pan and press down a bit, then cover with plastic wrap and refrigerate overnight or up to 24 hours.

5. When you're ready to bake, remove the plastic from the pan, place the pan in a cold oven, and heat the oven to 325°F. Cook until a knife inserted in the center of the strata comes out clean (it can be a little damp, but there shouldn't be wet egg mixture clinging to it), about 1 hour 15 minutes.

6. Let the strata rest for 5 to 10 minutes to allow the eggs to set. Serve warm or at room temperature.

Nonstick cooking spray or unsalted butter, melted, for the pan

2 ounces cream cheese, at room temperature

4 large eggs

$\frac{1}{2}$ ounce Parmesan cheese, grated

$\frac{1}{2}$ cup heavy cream

4 cups $\frac{1}{2}$-inch bread cubes

4 ounces Cheddar cheese, cut into $\frac{1}{4}$-inch cubes

4 ounces Monterey Jack cheese, cut into $\frac{1}{4}$-inch cubes

TIP

If the oven is already hot, you don't have to start in a cold oven—that's just a convenience for folks who don't want to wait for the oven to heat up. If you're cooking in a glass or ceramic pan, place it on a baking sheet to reduce the chance it will crack from thermal shock as it goes from refrigerator temperature to hot oven. Remove the plastic and bake at 325°F until a knife inserted in the center comes out clean, about 1 hour 10 minutes.

FRENCH TOAST

When I was a kid, my mom made a very basic French toast with store-bought bread, eggs, and milk. It was a no-frills sort of breakfast rather than something special. This French toast is a little more decadent and a little more suited for special occasions. Try it with Cinnamon Swirl Bread (p. 48), Rustic Sourdough Bread (p. 13), or Bacon, Tomato, and Cheddar Loaf (p. 14), or any of the white or wheat breads.

SERVES 2

1. Combine the eggs, crème fraîche, salt, and vanilla extract in a shallow bowl.

2. Soak the bread in the egg mixture while you melt the butter in a sauté pan on medium heat. Let the butter continue heating until it just begins to brown, then place the bread in the pan. Cook on the first side until the bread is browned, then flip and cook on the second side. Serve hot.

3 large eggs
¼ cup crème fraîche
½ teaspoon kosher salt
1 teaspoon pure vanilla extract
2 to 3 slices bread
2 tablespoons unsalted butter

TIP

If you don't have crème fraîche, you can use sour cream, yogurt, or milk.

MONTE CARLA SANDWICH

While I was writing this book, my friend Carla followed my progress, asked questions, and made suggestions. One day, she asked if I was going to name a recipe after her. I'd already been thinking about making a version of a Monte Cristo sandwich, and I knew it needed a name. Thus, the Monte Carla.

This is a great way to use up leftover French toast—or make the French toast specifically for this sandwich.

SERVES 1

Pile the ham, strawberry slices, and cheese on one slice of French toast, then top with the second slice. Cook in a sandwich press, on a griddle, or in a sauté pan, flipping the sandwich to warm it on both sides. It's done when the cheese is melted and the ham is warm. Serve hot.

3 thin slices deli ham
1 large strawberry, sliced thin
2 slices Gruyère or similar cheese
2 slices French toast

TIP

If strawberries aren't in season, use jam, jelly, or cranberry sauce. For something different, try thinly sliced apples.

HAM *and* APPLE STRATA

The name strata refers to layers, but I think it really means, "I need to feed a bunch of people but don't want to wake up and make pancakes endlessly." A close cousin of bread pudding, French toast, and the bread stuffing you put into your Thanksgiving turkey, stratas can accommodate a large variety of ingredients, so they're perfect for feeding a crowd. Make several different stratas, serve some fresh fruit and coffee, and breakfast is done.

Stratas are also great for using up leftover or slightly stale bread. Hearty homemade breads are perfect, but when it comes to flavors, you can mix and match—use what you have, as long as the flavors are compatible. This strata would be great with some rye bread along with white, or even with some sweet cubes, like the Maple Sugar and Candied Walnut Swirl Bread (p. 55).

Since it's best for the strata to rest overnight while the eggs soak into the bread, it makes cooking even easier. All you have to do in the morning is put the casserole in the oven, turn the oven on, and sit back and relax until the food is done.

SERVES 6 TO 8

1. Melt the butter in a small sauté pan. Add the apples, salt, and ground cloves (if using), and cook, stirring as needed, until the apples are cooked through, about 4 minutes. Set aside.

2. Combine the milk, eggs, and pepper in a small bowl. Beat to combine.

3. Place about a third of the bread cubes in the bottom of a 2-quart casserole dish, then spread half of the apples and half of the ham over the top. Add one more layer of bread and top with the remaining apples and ham. Top with the remaining bread.

4. Pour the milk and egg mixture evenly over the top of the bread cubes. Press down to make sure all the cubes are submerged. If any of the bread cubes look a little dry, pour a little extra milk over the top. Cover the pan with plastic wrap and refrigerate overnight or up to 24 hours.

5. When you're ready to bake, remove the plastic from the pan, place the pan in a cold oven, and heat the oven to 325°F. Cook until a knife inserted in the center of the strata comes out clean (it can be a little damp, but there shouldn't be wet egg mixture clinging to it), about 1 hour 15 minutes.

6. Let the strata rest for 5 to 10 minutes to allow the eggs to set. Serve warm or at room temperature.

2 tablespoons unsalted butter

2 firm baking apples, peeled and cut into large dice

Pinch of kosher salt

Pinch of ground cloves (optional)

1 cup milk

6 large eggs

1/2 teaspoon ground white pepper

6 cups 1/2-inch bread cubes

1 cup diced ham

FRENCH ONION SOUP STRATA

If you like French onion soup, you'll love this strata. It's the solid version, with the bread, the cheese, and onions, with sage adding an herby, savory flavor.

Use any white, wheat, or rye bread (or a mix) in this strata. You can use white or yellow onions, and if you want a little color, add a scallion as well. Although I love red onions, I don't suggest using them here. The color changes to gray and doesn't look very appealing.

No Gruyère? Use Swiss or any good melting cheese like Monterey Jack or mozzarella. It won't be exactly the same, but it will still be good.

SERVES 4

1. Melt the butter in a medium sauté pan and cook the onions until they're soft and translucent, 5 to 6 minutes. Let cool.

2. Add the eggs, milk, salt, and sage to a large bowl; whisk to combine. Add the onions and bread cubes and stir to moisten the bread. Transfer the bread mixture to a 1-quart casserole and top with the cheese. Press the mixture down a bit to make sure all the bread is moistened, then cover the casserole with plastic wrap and refrigerate overnight or up to 24 hours.

3. When you're ready to bake, remove the plastic from the pan, place the pan in a cold oven, and heat the oven to 325°F. Cook until a knife inserted in the center of the strata comes out clean (it can be a little damp, but there shouldn't be wet egg mixture clinging to it), about 1 hour 15 minutes.

4. Let the strata rest for 5 to 10 minutes to allow the eggs to set. Serve warm or at room temperature.

2 tablespoons unsalted butter

2 medium onions, diced

3 large eggs

1 cup milk

1/2 teaspoon kosher salt

1/2 teaspoon dried ground sage

4 cups 1/2-inch bread cubes

4 ounces Gruyère cheese, sliced or shredded

TIP

If you want to add a meaty flavor, sauté some mushrooms with the onions.

MAPLE PECAN BREAD PUDDING

Maple and pecans are a natural pair, but walnuts would also be a good choice in this bread pudding. If you can't find grade B maple syrup, which has more maple flavor, you can use grade A syrup instead. Use sourdough, any white or wheat loaf or bun, Cinnamon Swirl Bread (p. 48), or Strawberry Jam Swirl Loaf (p. 59) for this bread pudding.

You can serve the bread pudding in their ramekins or unmold them before serving (run a knife around the inside of the ramekin, then invert the puddings onto serving plates).

SERVES 4

1. Heat the oven to 325°F.

2. In a medium bowl, whisk together the milk, eggs, maple syrup, vanilla extract, and salt. Add the pecans and bread cubes and stir. Let them sit for a few moments to absorb the liquid. Portion the bread and liquid into four 1-cup ramekins. If desired, sprinkle some Vanilla Sugar on top of the bread puddings. You can cook the puddings immediately or wait until the bread has absorbed even more of the liquid. Or, cover and refrigerate and bake later.

3. When ready to bake, place the ramekins in a casserole dish or baking pan and fill the pan with hot, nearly boiling water to about halfway up the sides of the ramekins. Place the pan in the oven and bake the puddings until they puff up and a knife inserted in the center of one comes out mostly clean, about 50 minutes. It's fine if there's a bit of cooked custard on the knife, but it shouldn't be wet and liquidy.

5. Carefully remove the ramekins from the hot water and serve warm.

1 cup milk

4 large eggs

$\frac{1}{2}$ cup grade B maple syrup

1 tablespoon pure vanilla extract

$\frac{1}{2}$ teaspoon kosher salt

$\frac{1}{2}$ cup chopped pecans

4 cups $\frac{1}{2}$-inch bread cubes

Vanilla Sugar (p. 189), optional

TIP

Want something even more decadent? Serve a scoop of ice cream on top of the hot bread pudding.

INDIVIDUAL STUFFED FRENCH TOAST *with* CREAM CHEESE *and* FRESH RASPBERRIES

Standard French toast starts with slices of bread, but it doesn't have to. A bun or dinner roll is perfect for this recipe—it leaves plenty of space for the savory cream cheese inside. For a sweeter French toast, you could use a sweet bun.

The sweet-tartness of the raspberries plays counterpoint to the richness of the French toast. If berries aren't in season, a few frozen berries or some jam would be just as nice.

If you're feeding a crowd, feel free to cook a number of buns or rolls in a casserole dish.

SERVES 1

1. Heat the oven to 325°F.

2. Fit a bun neatly inside a 1-cup ramekin, leaving just a little space around the outside for the extra liquid. If your bun is wider than the ramekin, just trim off the outside so it will fit. Remove the bun from the ramekin, cut it in half horizontally, then spread cream cheese on the bottom half.

3. In a small bowl, whisk together the egg, cream, and salt. Pour a little of the mixture into the ramekin, then put the bottom of the bun in the ramekin. Pour in a little more of the egg mixture, add the bun top, then pour the rest of the egg mixture on top. If it doesn't all fit, press down a bit on the bun to encourage it to absorb more liquid. Let the bun sit in the liquid for 10 to 20 minutes to absorb the liquid, or refrigerate for several hours or until the next day, if you prefer.

4. Put the ramekin in a larger pan or casserole and add hot, nearly boiling water to the pan to about halfway up the ramekin. Place the pan in the oven and bake until the bun puffs up and a knife inserted in the center comes out clean, about 45 minutes. It's fine if there's a bit of cheese on the knife, but it shouldn't be wet and liquidy.

5. Remove the pan from the oven and carefully remove the ramekin from the hot water.

6. Invert the French toast onto a serving plate or keep in the ramekin. Top the French toast with as many fresh raspberries as you like. You can also sprinkle with a bit of confectioners' sugar if you like.

1 bun or dinner roll
2 tablespoons cream cheese, at room temperature
1 large egg
1/4 cup heavy cream
Pinch of kosher salt
Fresh raspberries
Confectioners' sugar, for garnish (optional)

TIP

The recipe calls for heavy cream, which makes a very rich French toast, but you can substitute milk for the cream, if you like.

SAUSAGE *and* CHEDDAR STRATA

If you can find bulk breakfast sausage, it eliminates a step, but you can also buy link breakfast sausage and remove it from the casings before cooking. If you happen to have cooked, leftover breakfast sausage, you can use that for this dish as well (you'll need about a cup of cooked sausage).

Use any white, wheat, or rye bread for this strata. It's also a good use for leftover dinner rolls or hamburger or hot dog buns. Try the Stuffing Bread with Dried Cranberries (p. 38) or Yeasted Jalapeño and Roasted Red Pepper Cornbread (p. 41) for something really tasty.

Since the sausage is well seasoned, you won't need any additional salt or spices.

SERVES 4 TO 6

1. Cook the sausage in a medium sauté pan, breaking it up a bit as it cooks—you don't want it completely crumbled, but you don't want huge chunks either. Cook until no trace of pink remains, then let it cool completely.

2. Combine the milk and eggs in a small bowl. Beat to combine.

3. Place about half of the bread cubes in the bottom of a 1-quart casserole dish, then spread the sausage evenly over the bread. Top with about half of the cubed cheese. Put the rest of the bread on top of the meat and cheese and top with the rest of the cheese cubes.

4. Pour the egg mixture evenly over the top of the bread cubes. Press down to make sure all the cubes are evenly moistened. If any bread cubes look a little dry, pour a little extra milk over the top. Cover the pan with plastic wrap and refrigerate overnight or up to 24 hours.

5. When you're ready to bake, remove the plastic from the pan, place the pan in a cold oven, and heat the oven to 325°F. Cook until a knife inserted in the center of the strata comes out clean (it can be a little damp, but there shouldn't be wet egg mixture clinging to it), about 1 hour 15 minutes.

6. Let the strata rest for 5 to 10 minutes to allow the eggs to set. Serve warm or at room temperature.

1/2 pound bulk breakfast sausage

1/2 cup milk, half-and-half, or heavy cream

5 large eggs

4 cups 1/2-inch bread cubes

4 ounces Cheddar cheese, cut into 1/4-inch cubes

TIP

For a heartier dish, add another 1/2 pound layer of cooked sausage on top of the strata and top with a thin layer of shredded cheese.

SPINACH *and* LEEK STRATA

Depending on where they're grown, leeks can be very gritty or just a little dirty, but they always need to be cleaned before you cook them. Cut them in half lengthwise and rinse the dirt from between the layers, or you can cut them into smaller pieces first, then rinse well. It's best to rinse in a bowl of water, swishing the leeks around, then remove them from the dirty water and rinse again the same way.

If you can't find leeks, onions or shallots would make a fine substitution. Use any white, wheat, or rye loaf, or a combination. Also try the Mini Sunflower Seed Loaves (p. 26) or the Sauerkraut Rye (p. 32).

This strata looks pretty served in a ceramic pie dish and cut into wedges for serving.

SERVES 4 TO 6

1. Melt the butter in a medium sauté pan and cook the leeks until translucent and tender, 3 to 4 minutes. Set aside to cool to room temperature.

2. Combine the cool leeks, spinach, eggs, cream, buttermilk, salt, and pepper in a large bowl. Stir or whisk to break up the eggs. Add the bread cubes and mix well.

3. Transfer the mixture to an 8-inch ceramic pie pan or 1-quart casserole dish. Cover the pan with plastic wrap and refrigerate overnight or up to 24 hours.

4. When you're ready to bake, remove the plastic from the pan, place the pan in a cold oven, and heat the oven to 325°F. Cook until a knife inserted in the center of the strata comes out clean (it can be a little damp, but there shouldn't be wet egg mixture clinging to it), about 1 hour 15 minutes.

5. Let the strata rest for 5 to 10 minutes to allow the eggs to set. Serve warm or at room temperature.

2 tablespoons unsalted butter

2 leeks, white and light green parts, cleaned, quartered lengthwise, and cut into $1/2$-inch pieces

$1/2$ pound frozen chopped spinach, defrosted and drained well

4 large eggs

$1/2$ cup heavy cream

$1/2$ cup buttermilk

$1/2$ teaspoon kosher salt

Several generous grinds black pepper

4 cups $1/2$-inch bread cubes

TIP

If you want to add some herbs, try sage or nutmeg.

BUTTERS
&SPREADS

CINNAMON-SUGAR COMPOUND BUTTER

This buttery spread is nice on toast, melted on French toast, added to your morning oatmeal, or on top of cooked sweet potatoes or winter squash. It's especially good on the Oatmeal-Honey-Date Loaf on p. 16.

There are a number of different types of cinnamon available, if you look beyond the generic varieties sold at supermarkets (see the tip). It doesn't matter which one you choose for this butter, as long as it's one you like—and as long as it's not so old that it has lost its flavor.

If you like spice, a tiny pinch of cayenne would add an interesting note to the butter.

MAKES ½ CUP

1. Cut the butter into a few pieces and add it to your food processor. Add the brown sugar, cinnamon, and salt. Pulse a few times, then process until the spice and sugar are evenly distributed in the butter. You might need to stop and scrape down the sides of the food processor once or twice to make sure all the cinnamon is blended in. Alternatively, you could mash the spices into the butter with a fork; just make sure the butter doesn't soften so much that it melts.

2. Transfer the butter to a storage container and refrigerate. The butter improves after a day, as the cinnamon absorbs moisture from the butter, enhancing the flavor. Use the butter within 2 weeks.

1 stick unsalted butter
2 tablespoons packed
    brown sugar
2 teaspoons ground cinnamon
Pinch of kosher salt

TIP

There are two types of cinnamon— cassia cinnamon, which is sweeter, and Ceylon, or "true" cinnamon, which is more complex with citrus notes. When you buy cinnamon without any indication of what type it is, it's likely to be cassia. But if you shop at spice stores and specialty markets, you'll find cinnamon varieties grown in different countries with different flavors. There's no wrong choice when it comes to cinnamon—choose the one you like best.

CHUNKY APPLE *and* CINNAMON SPREAD

This is a cross between a chunky jam, a pie filling, and an apple-sauce. It's great warm or cold, spread on bread or toast (try it on the Mini Sunflower Seed Loaves on p. 26), mixed into yogurt or oatmeal, or simply eaten with a spoon.

Cinnamon is a very common partner for apples, but in this case I wanted the apples to shine, so I added vanilla to balance the cinnamon and enhance the flavor of the apples.

MAKES 1 CUP

2 tablespoons unsalted butter

3 Granny Smith apples, peeled, cored, and cut into small dice

Pinch of kosher salt

1½ teaspoons ground cinnamon

¼ cup brown sugar

1 teaspoon pure vanilla extract

1. Melt the butter in a medium sauté pan over medium-high heat. Add the apples and toss to coat with the butter.

2. Add the salt, cinnamon, and brown sugar and continue cooking. The apples will release some liquid, then it will begin to evaporate. When the liquid is mostly gone, the apples are soft, and the mixture is thick (this will take about 10 minutes), take the pan off the heat and add the vanilla extract. Stir to combine, then transfer the mixture to a storage container and refrigerate. Use the apple spread within 1 week.

CHIVE CREAM CHEESE

My mother was a good cook when it came to preparing meals for the family, but she had some decidedly odd tastes when it came to her personal snacks. One of her favorites was rye bread with a smear of cream cheese and a slice of raw onion.

Now, while all those flavors go well together, the odd part was the huge slice of onion she would put on that innocent bread and cheese. When I was a kid, it didn't seem that odd because it's what I grew up with. Now I realize that the onion-to-everything ratio was a bit skewed.

This simple cream cheese and chive spread has the same flavors as Mom's snack, but in better proportions. I like this on the Sauerkraut Rye (see p. 32).

MAKES 1 CUP

1. Combine the cream cheese and milk in a small bowl, stirring until smooth. Add more milk, if needed, to bring it to a spreading consistency.

2. Add 1 tablespoon of the chives, along with the white pepper and lemon zest or juice. Mix well to combine. Taste and add more chives, if you prefer. Transfer to a storage container and refrigerate. The cream cheese will keep for 1 week.

8 ounces cream cheese, at room temperature

1 tablespoon milk, plus more as needed

1 to 2 tablespoons thinly sliced fresh chives

A few grinds of white pepper

1/2 teaspoon lemon zest or juice

TIP

This is best made at least 12 hours before serving to mellow the chive flavor and allow the flavors to combine.

BLACKBERRY COMPOUND BUTTER

This butter is a beautiful purple color with the flavor of berries. It's surprisingly solid when chilled, so be sure to take it out of the refrigerator before using if you want a spreadable consistency.

Besides using the butter for the typical breakfast breads, pancakes, or waffles, spread a thin layer on bread for a roast beef sandwich or brush some on chicken or pork chops while they're cooking on the grill.

MAKES 1½ CUPS

1. Cook the berries and sugar in a small saucepan on medium heat, stirring as needed until the berries are soft, about 5 minutes. Pass the mixture through a fine-mesh sieve to remove the seeds.

2. Transfer the purée back to the pan and continue cooking on medium heat, stirring often, until the mixture reduces to about ½ cup, 10 to 15 minutes. Allow the mixture to cool to room temperature.

3. Cut the butter into chunks and place in a food processor fitted with the metal blade (or you can do this in a medium bowl with an electric mixer). Process until the butter is smooth, then add the berry purée and continue processing, scraping down the bowl as needed, until completely combined.

4. Transfer to a storage container and refrigerate until needed. You can also form this into a log, wrap tightly in plastic, and slice when ready to use. The butter will keep for 1 week.

10 ounces fresh or frozen blackberries
½ cup sugar
2 sticks salted butter

TIP

You can make other berry butters using the same method. Raspberries are especially good.

CHOCOLATE BUTTER

When spread on toast, this butter will have you swooning. Try a thin layer on bread for your peanut butter sandwich or smear on a graham cracker. It's decadent when melted on waffles or pancakes.

This butter is very solid when chilled, so take it out of the refrigerator and let it come to room temperature if you need a spreadable consistency.

MAKES ¾ CUP

1. Put the cream and chocolate chips in a microwave-safe container and microwave for 15 seconds. Stir. The chips should be melted completely and combined with the cream. If there are still some unmelted chips, continue to microwave for 5 seconds at a time, as needed, stirring each time. The goal is to heat the mixture as little as possible and just melt the chips. Let the chocolate cool to room temperature.

2. Cut the butter into chunks and place in a food processor fitted with the metal blade. (You can also do this in a medium bowl with an electric hand mixer.) Process until the butter is smooth, then add the chocolate mixture and continue processing, scraping down the bowl as needed, until completely combined.

3. Transfer to a container and refrigerate. You can also form this into a log, wrap in plastic, and slice when ready to use. The butter will keep for 1 week.

1 tablespoon heavy cream
¼ cup semisweet chocolate chips
1 stick salted butter

TIP

Try this recipe with white chocolate—the method is the same.

CINNAMON HONEY

You can buy flavored honey, but it's simple to make. Since you're adding flavor, you don't need to splurge on a super-expensive honey, either. Save the fancy wildflower honey to use all by itself.

Besides using this as a spread on bread or a drizzle on pancakes or waffles, try it drizzled over fresh fruit, stirred into yogurt, or added to your hot or iced tea.

MAKES ½ CUP

1. Put the cinnamon sticks and honey in a small saucepan and heat on low just until the honey begins to bubble. Turn off the heat and transfer to a half-pint jar. Add more honey to top off the jar.

2. Cover and let cool. Store at room temperature and use within 4 weeks.

4 sticks (about 3 to 4 inches long) cinnamon
½ cup honey

TIP

If you don't use this up quickly, you can keep replenishing the honey in the jar as you use it—those cinnamon sticks will continue releasing flavor. If you find that the new honey isn't quite as flavorful, heat it with the cinnamon sticks, just like the first time.

MAPLE COMPOUND BUTTER

Compound butters are nice to have on hand to make morning toast or oatmeal a little more special. They're incredibly simple to make, so there's no reason not to have three or four at the same time. A variety is especially nice on a brunch table.

Use honey in place of the maple syrup, if you like.

MAKES ½ CUP

1. Put the butter in a food processor fitted with the metal blade and process until smooth (or add the butter to a medium bowl and use a hand-held electric mixer). Add the maple syrup and salt and blend until combined.

2. Transfer to a container and refrigerate. You can also form this into a log, wrap in plastic, and slice. Use the butter within 1 week.

1 stick unsalted butter, at room temperature
2 tablespoons grade B maple syrup
¼ teaspoon kosher salt

TIP

Compound butters freeze well, so make them ahead and freeze what you won't use immediately.

ORANGE *and* GINGER COMPOUND BUTTER

I love citrus, and pairing it with ginger is a natural combination. Besides putting this on your toast or muffins, try it on pork or chicken.

MAKES ½ CUP

1. Put the butter in a food processor fitted with the metal blade and process until smooth (or add the butter to a medium bowl and use a hand-held electric mixer). Add the orange oil, ginger, and salt and blend until combined.

2. Transfer to a container and refrigerate. You can also form this into a log, wrap in plastic, and slice when ready to use. Use the butter within 1 week.

1 stick unsalted butter
¼ teaspoon pure orange oil
¼ teaspoon grated fresh ginger
¼ teaspoon kosher salt

TIP

Lemon or lime oils are also great combined with butter.

APPLE *and* SAGE COMPOUND BUTTER

This is a perfect butter for fall, with apples and sage making this sweet, tart, and savory.

The flavor of the apple is quite strong, so pick one that you like—tart or sweet. A baking apple (such as Honey Crisp or Pink Lady) that stays firm when cooked will give you a butter with more texture than an apple that disintegrates into a sauce (such as Braeburn or Cortland). Either is fine, so choose one based on what you want the end result to be.

Besides being delicious slathered on French toast or waffles, this butter is great with pork dishes, either on your dinner roll or melted on top of a pork chop during cooking. It's also good melted atop winter squash.

MAKES 1 CUP

1. Melt 1 tablespoon of butter in a sauté pan. Add the apple and sage and cook, stirring as needed, until the apples are cooked through and soft, about 10 minutes. Remove the pan from the heat and let the apples cool completely.

2. Put the stick of butter in a food processor fitted with the metal blade and process until smooth (or add the butter to a medium bowl and use a hand-held electric mixer). Add the cooled apples, white pepper, salt, and cream cheese. Blend until combined. Taste for seasoning and add more salt, if desired. If the apples are too chunky for your liking, continue processing until you like the texture.

3. Transfer to a container and refrigerate. You can also form this into a log, wrap in plastic, and slice when ready to use. The butter will keep for 1 week.

1 stick unsalted butter, plus 1 tablespoon, divided

1 apple, peeled, cored, and cut into small dice

1/4 teaspoon ground sage

1/4 teaspoon ground white pepper

1/4 teaspoon kosher salt, plus more as needed

1 ounce (2 tablespoons) cream cheese, at room temperature

TIP

Replace the sage with cinnamon and a dash of nutmeg or clove for an apple pie–like flavored butter.

BALSAMIC *and* OLIVE OIL
DIPPING OIL *with* HERBS

The first time I went to a restaurant and a waiter poured balsamic vinegar, herbs, and oil into a shallow bowl, I wondered why. It sure looked like something I'd put on a salad.

Now I'm more sophisticated. Really, I just love an excuse to dip bread into lightly infused vinegar and oil. With or without lettuce nearby.

This dipping oil gets better as it sits as the herbs hydrate and the flavors combine. Make it ahead, if you have the time. Store the leftovers in the refrigerator if you'll be keeping them for more than a day or two. The olive oil is likely to thicken when it gets cold, but it will liquefy again at room temperature.

MAKES 3/4 CUP

In a small jar (1/2 pint is perfect), combine the water, salt, basil, rosemary, thyme, oregano, marjoram, garlic, and sugar. Let it sit for 5 minutes to begin hydrating the herbs. Add the vinegar and oil. Cover the jar and shake to combine. Pour into a shallow bowl for dipping.

2 tablespoons water
1/2 teaspoon kosher salt
1/2 teaspoon dried basil
1/4 teaspoon dried rosemary
1/4 teaspoon dried thyme
1/4 teaspoon dried oregano
1/4 teaspoon dried marjoram
1/4 teaspoon minced dried garlic
1 teaspoon sugar
2 tablespoons balsamic vinegar
1/2 cup extra-virgin olive oil

TIP

You can also use sherry or wine vinegar instead of the balsamic.

SWEET CHEESE *with* CINNAMON

Sometimes you just want a smear of cheese, right? But cheese isn't always savory. This sweetened cheese isn't overly sweet, with cinnamon adding some warmth.

This is a natural on an English muffin, the Gluten-Free Seed and Nut Bread on p. 31 or the Whole Wheat Cloverleaf Rolls on p. 89. For something different, stir it into mashed winter squash.

MAKES 1 CUP

1. Combine all of the ingredients (start with 4 tablespoons of sugar) in a food processor, and process until smooth (or add to a medium bowl and use a hand-held electric mixer). Taste and add more sugar, if desired.

2. Transfer to a small storage container and refrigerate. This will be somewhat loose right after processing, but it will firm up after it is chilled. Use within 1 week.

6 ounces cream cheese, at room temperature

4 ounces ricotta cheese

4 to 6 tablespoons sugar

1 teaspoon ground cinnamon

1 teaspoon kosher salt

TIP

While I like the combination of cream cheese mixed with ricotta, you could use all of one or the other. If you like the tartness, you could substitute both with chèvre (and spread on toasted baguette slices as a snack). Drained or dry cottage cheese would also work well.

VANILLA SUGAR

Vanilla sugar is expensive, so make your own. It's great to keep on hand to top sweet breads or muffins before you bake them, to sprinkle on your morning cereal or oatmeal, or to stir into coffee or tea. It's also a great way to use the empty pod after you've used fresh vanilla beans in another recipe.

MAKES 1 QUART

IF USING VANILLA BEANS

1. After you've removed the vanilla beans from the pod, for another use, put the pod in a container with the sugar (make sure the container has a tight-fitting lid). If you used your vanilla pod in a recipe that required steeping the pod in liquid, simply rinse the used pod, let it dry, and then put it in the container of sugar. Over time, the sugar will absorb the vanilla flavor.

2. When you use some of the vanilla sugar, just add more plain sugar and shake the container to mix it. You can also put split fresh vanilla beans in the sugar, if you like.

IF USING VANILLA EXTRACT

1. Put the sugar in a small bowl, add the vanilla extract, and stir until the sugar is evenly moistened with the extract. Store in a closed container.

2. If you leave the container open, the liquid will evaporate and you'll have a dry sugar. Stir it once in a while as it dries so it doesn't form chunks and clumps; store in a closed container once the liquid has evaporated, 1 to 2 days.

IF USING VANILLA BEANS

1 vanilla bean pod (or use more as you have them)

4 cups (1 quart) sugar

IF USING VANILLA EXTRACT

1 cup sugar

1 tablespoon pure vanilla extract

TIP

Try different brands of vanilla extract and different sources for your beans—there are a lot of varieties and some pretty surprising differences in flavor.

HOMEMADE BUTTER

I don't make butter often, but I sometimes like to serve it with my homemade bread and impress my guests. It's quite easy to do—a machine does all the work. If you like, use this homemade butter as the basis for other butter and spread recipes here.

A pint of heavy cream will yield less than a stick of butter, along with the liquid that is the original "buttermilk." It's not the same as the buttermilk we buy today, because that product is cultured, but the liquid left over from butter making is actually pretty tasty. You can use it where you'd use a milk product—in cooking or baking, or even in hot chocolate.

MAKES LESS THAN 1 STICK

1 pint heavy cream
Pinch of kosher salt

1. Put the cream and salt in a blender or in a stand mixer fitted with the whisk attachment. (A blender works better in keeping the splatters contained.)

2. Turn on the machine and let it run. You'll see the cream turn into whipped cream, then lumps and a thin liquid will form, then lumps of butter, and finally chunks of butter. The whole process takes about 5 minutes.

3. Taste and add more salt if needed. Unsalted butter will keep for about a week; salted butter lasts a bit longer.

NUT *or* SEED BUTTER

Nut butters of all types are easy to make at home. And if you make them yourself, you can control how much salt and sugar you add. I like a tiny pinch of salt, but I seldom add sugar because I want the flavor of the nuts to shine.

Another advantage to making your own nut butters is that you can create flavor combinations—peanuts and cashews are great together, for example. Both roasted and raw nuts can be used for nut butters; again, look for unsalted products and add your own salt, to taste.

For folks who can't have nuts, seed butters are a great alternative. Sunflower or pumpkin seeds make great nut-free butters.

You'll get about half as much nut butter—or less—than the amount of nuts you started with, so keep that in mind.

MAKES ABOUT 1 CUP

1. Put the nuts, salt, and a pinch of sugar, if desired, in a food processor fitted with the metal blade. Pulse a few times, then process, scraping down the processor as needed. (Depending on your model, you might be able to make nut butter in your blender. Some are more successful at the task than others.) First, you'll have chopped nuts, then powdery nuts. It doesn't take too long before the nuts start looking a little clumpy, like wet sand. Then they gather together in a ball. Eventually the mixture will smooth out and become a smooth nut butter. Taste and add another pinch or two of sugar if desired, processing to incorporate.

2. Transfer the butter to a storage container and use within 2 weeks. Like the natural nut butters on the market, if you leave this stored for a while, the oil will rise to the top. Just mix it back in before using.

2 cups nuts
Pinch of salt
Sugar (optional)

TIP

If you want a chunky product, chop or pulse the nuts to your desired consistency, and set those aside to add to the nut butter after it is finished.

STONE FRUIT *and* ALMOND JAM

I love the flavor of peaches and almond together, which is the inspiration for this jam. You can use any stone fruits you like. Peaches, plums, apricots, or nectarines would be my choice.

When these fruits are in season, choose those with no bumps or bruises, though it's fine if they are a little under-ripe. When stone fruits are out of season, you can find them frozen. Better yet, freeze some extra when the fruit is in season and then you can make this jam year-round.

3 cups stone fruit, such as peaches, nectarines, apricots, or plums

1/2 cup sugar

1/4 teaspoon kosher salt

1 teaspoon pure vanilla extract

1/2 teaspoon almond extract

2 tablespoons instant pectin

MAKES 1 PINT

1. Peel the fruit. You can use a serrated peeler or cut an X in the bottom of the fruit and blanch in a pot of boiling water for 30 seconds, then transfer to a bowl of ice water. You should be able to slip off the skin. Cut open the fruit, remove the pit, and chop the flesh into 1/4-inch dice.

2. Place the chopped fruit, sugar, and salt in a medium saucepan and cook over medium heat until most of the water is gone, the fruit is soft, and the mixture has thickened a bit, 10 to 20 minutes depending on what kind of fruit you used.

3. Take the pan off the heat and stir in the extracts. Let it cool to room temperature, then stir in the pectin. Stir well, then transfer to a storage container and refrigerate. Use the jam within a week.

WINE JAM

This jam is perfect for leftover wine. Any wine will work—white or red. If you like to drink it, you will like it for this jam.

When you cook the wine, much of the alcohol boils out and the raw wine taste mellows so you end up with a softer flavor. Once you've made this jam a few times, have fun experimenting by adding accent flavors—a bit of mint, a little bit of orange juice, or some vanilla extract can be lovely.

Instant pectin is one of my favorite kitchen secrets. Unlike traditional pectin used for jam and jelly making, it doesn't need to be heated and it doesn't require a lot of sugar, either. If you ever need a stable whipped cream that doesn't deflate, add a bit of instant pectin as you finish whipping and it will last for days in the refrigerator.

1 cup wine
1/4 cup sugar
1 teaspoon fresh lemon juice
Zest of 1/2 lemon
2 tablespoons instant pectin

MAKES 1 PINT

1. Put the wine and sugar in a small saucepan and bring to a boil, stirring as needed to dissolve the sugar. Reduce to a simmer and cook for 2 minutes.

2. Remove the pan from the heat and add the lemon juice and zest. Let the mixture cool to room temperature, then stir in the instant pectin. Pour into a pint jar, cover, and refrigerate. Use within 2 weeks.

METRIC EQUIVALENTS

Liquid/Dry Measures

U.S.	Metric
1/4 teaspoon	1.25 milliliters
1/2 teaspoon	2.5 milliliters
1 teaspoon	5 milliliters
1 tablespoon (3 teaspoons)	15 milliliters
1 fluid ounce (2 tablespoons)	30 milliliters
1/4 cup	60 milliliters
1/3 cup	80 milliliters
1/2 cup	120 milliliters
1 cup	240 milliliters
1 pint (2 cups)	480 milliliters
1 quart (4 cups; 32 ounces)	960 milliliters
1 gallon (4 quarts)	3.84 liters
1 ounce (by weight)	28 grams
1 pound	454 grams
2.2 pounds	1 kilogram

Oven Temperatures

°F	Gas Mark	°C
250	1/2	120
275	1	140
300	2	150
325	3	165
350	4	180
375	5	190
400	6	200
425	7	220
450	8	230
475	9	240
500	10	260
550	Broil	290

VOLUME *to* WEIGHT CONVERSIONS *for* COMMONLY USED INGREDIENTS

Ingredient	Volume	U.S. Weight	Metric Weight
Butter	1 tablespoon	$1/2$ ounce	14 grams
Flour (all but semolina and gluten-free)	1 cup	$4^1/2$ ounces	128 grams
Flour (semolina)	1 cup	6 ounces	170 grams
Flour (gluten-free multipurpose, King Arthur brand)	1 cup	$5^1/2$ ounces	156 grams
Hazelnut meal	1 cup	$3^1/8$ ounces	89 grams
Honey	1 tablespoon	$3/4$ ounce	21 grams
Instant mashed potato flakes	1 cup	2 ounces	57 grams
Jam	1 cup	12 ounces	340 grams
Maple sugar	1 cup	$5^1/2$ ounces	156 grams
Maple syrup	1 cup	11 ounces	312 grams
Nonfat dry milk	1 cup	3 ounces	85 grams
Nut butter	1 cup	$9^1/2$ ounces	269 grams
Nuts, chopped	1 cup	4 ounces	113 grams
Oats, quick-cooking	1 cup	$3^1/8$ ounces	89 grams
Oil	1 cup	7 ounces	200 grams
Pine nuts	1 cup	5 ounces	142 grams
Salt, Morton kosher	1 teaspoon	0.21 ounce	6 grams
Sunflower seeds	1 cup	5 ounces	142 grams
Sugar, brown	1 cup	$7^1/2$ ounces	212 grams
Sugar, white	1 cup	7 ounces	200 grams
Tomatoes, sun-dried	1 cup	6 ounces	170 grams
Yeast, active dry	2.25 teaspoons	$1/4$ ounce	7 grams

RESOURCES

ANOLON®
Bakeware
www.anolon.com

BOB'S RED MILL
Flours and other ingredients
www.bobsredmill.com

CAKE BOSS™ CAKEWARE COLLECTIONS
Bakeware and kitchen tools
www.cakebossbaking.com

CUISINART
Food processors and kitchen tools
www.cuisinart.com

EMILE HENRY®
Dutch ovens and baking dishes
www.emilehenryusa.com

GOOD COOK
Bakeware and kitchen tools
www.goodcook.com

HODGSON MILL
Flours
www.hodgsonmill.com

KING ARTHUR FLOUR
Flours and other ingredients, bakeware, and kitchen tools
www.kingarthurflour.com

KITCHENAID
Stand mixers, food processors, and kitchen tools
www.kitchenaid.com

LE CREUSET®
Dutch ovens and baking dishes
www.lecreuset.com

LODGE MANUFACTURING®
Cast-iron pans, Dutch ovens, and griddles
www.lodgemfg.com

MAGIMIX
Food processors
www.magimix.com

MICROPLANE®
Zesters and graters
www.microplane.com

NORDIC WARE®
Bakeware
www.nordicware.com

OXO®
Kitchen tools
www.oxo.com

RED STAR YEAST
Yeast
www.redstaryeast.com

SILPAT®
Baking mats
www.silpat.com

SUR LA TABLE®
Bakeware, ingredients, and kitchen tools
www.surlatable.com

THERMOWORKS®
Thermometers and timers
www.thermoworks.com

WILLIAMS-SONOMA®
Bakeware, ingredients, and kitchen tools
www.williams-sonoma.com

WÜSTHOF
Knives
www.wuesthof.com

INDEX

Numbers in bold indicate pages with photographs

If you like this book, you'll love *Fine Cooking*.